AF856190

The valuation of goods for customs purposes

'Anything to declare?'
'Only my genius.'
Oscar Wilde versus US customs.

The valuation of goods for customs purposes

by

HENK DE PAGTER

and

RICHARD VAN RAAN

1981
Springer Science+Business Media, LLC

Translated by J.W. Reintjes

Cover design: Pieter J. van der Sman

ISBN 978-94-017-4512-3 ISBN 978-94-017-4510-9 (eBook)
DOI 10.1007/978-94-017-4510-9

© 1981 Springer Science+Business Media New York
Originally published by Kluwer, Deventer, The Netherlands in 1981
Softcover reprint of the hardcover 1st edition 1981

All rights reserved. No part of this publication may be reproduced, stored in a retrieval system, or transmitted in any form by any means, electronic, mechanical, photocopying, recording or otherwise, without the prior written permission of the publisher.

Preface

This book was written in response to the coming into force on the first of January 1981 of the Customs Valuation Code of the GATT, an agreement which has been applied unilaterally by the EEC and the US since the first of July 1980.

As a result of the new agreement a uniform system for the valuation of goods for customs purposes will be used for the first time in history of international trade by the most important trading nations. This can be seen as an important step in the removal of trade barriers, as the use of a uniform system enables anyone occupied with international trade to foresee with reasonable accuracy the treatment he will receive in other countries.

This book provides a survey of the new system, together with the application and interpretation which to our opinion may be expected on the basis of the international discussions. Some attention is paid, moreover, to the remaining systems of valuation of goods which the exporter may encounter.

In writing this book we have not only had the aim of providing a source of information for exporters, but we believe it will be of use to anyone who is, or has to be, interested in the customs valuation.

March 1981, the authors.

Richard van Raan, after studying civil law at the university of Leiden, specialised himself in fiscal law.

Henk de Pagter studied fiscal law in Rotterdam.

Both are at present employed by the Ministry of Finance and occupied with national and international customs legislation. They participated in the GATT-discussions on the new customs valuation at Geneva and in its development in the EEC.

Contents

Chapter 1. Introduction

On the first of July 1980 the EEC and the US introduced new systems of valuation of goods for customs purposes. On the first of January 1981 they were followed in this by Finland, Hong-Kong, Japan, Norway, Austria, Sweden and Switzerland, and in the near future several other countries will similarly renew their legislation on this subject (e.g. Australia, the first of July 1981). If expectations are justified, all of this is the beginning of a new era in the field of customs valuation.

What is the meaning of 'customs valuation'? When import duties are not levied according to a fixed standard (e.g. m^3, hl, or kg) they are levied to the value of a product. Combinations of both standards may also occur. When the value of a product is taken as the standard, it of course becomes necessary to clarify this concept. Even if the trade-price of the goods is taken as a starting-point, one has to draw up certain rules in order to avoid, as far as possible, treating importers differently, in spite of different methods of invoicing. Together, these rules make up the system of valuation used by the customs service on the importation of goods which leads to the customs value, the value which is used for the calculation of import duties.

The customs-value found in this manner may, or may not, match normal trade-practice. The former is the case when the price paid is taken as far as possible as the customs value, with only a few adjustments (e.g. addition of costs of transport and insurance not included in the price) to avoid distorting the conditions of competition. The latter is the case, however, when the customs value is independently fixed by the customs service, disregarding the price paid, on the basis of e.g. minimumprices or prices on the home-market. This course is dictated by fiscal- or protectionist policy. Both the rate of import duty and the system of customs valuation are instruments for pursuing fiscal and trade-political ends. The system of custons valuation is equally suited to protectionist purposes and the increase of income such as the raising of the rate of duty. By applying a system of valuation which has scarcely any relation to the price actually paid, it is possible to protect the home-market to a great extent, while the real pressure of import duty is considerably higher than is shown by the percentage by itself. Moreover, a change in the rate of import duty is clearly visible, while an increase in the rate of duty as a result of changes in the system of valuation is considerably less noticeable and more difficult to prove.

As a result, customs valuation practices may have quite a restrictive influence on international trade on account of the uncertainty as to the value over which the import duties will be calculated. Some have said that this uncertainty is more of a trade restriction than the import duties themselves.

The customs valuation is not only of interest for the levying of import duties, but is also used for levying other taxes on importation. In addition the customs valuation is often used in the writing off on import licences and import quota's as far as these are based on the value of goods.

This all explains why an attempt to arrive internationally at a uniform system of customs valuation was already made several decades ago. Especially for trade the advantages are obvious. With a more uniform system every exporter could, for instance, be quite sure of what to expect abroad. This would make it easier for him to enter other markets. The search for a uniform system, however, remained more or less a Utopian dream. It may be true that the so-called Brussels definition of value – a system internationally agreed upon – could lay claim to a lot of popularity, but in practice it left the countries using it a fair amount of room to manoeuvre. Besides, there were several other systems in use (e.g. in Mexico, Brazil and, until recently, the US and Australia), criticized by many for their aggressive nature.

In view of all this it is altogether understandable that this problem was brought forward during the multilateral trade negotiations held in Geneva from 1973 to 1979. These negotiations were aimed at removing both tariff and non tariff trade barriers as far as possible in international trade.

During one of the first meetings the question arose as to whether the existence of different systems of valuation for customs purposes alongside of each other should be qualified as a (non-tariff) trade barrier. This was affirmed by the EEC amongst others, but rejected by the US. Such a difference of opinion is not as strange as it may seem at first sight. By raising the question the EEC had in fact opened an attack on the American system of customs valuation (including the 'American Selling Price') – qualified as obscure and protectionist by many – as wel as on other aggressive systems. The countries in question (including the US and Canada) were initially of course not eager to include systems of customs valuation in the negotiations. Eventually, however, they declared themselves willing to negotiate on this matter, with the proviso 'there are no free lunches'. This meant they regarded the abandoning of their system as a trade-political concession for which the EEC should offer other concessions (e.g. in tariffs).

This development made the customs valuation one of the most important objects of negotiation of the Tokyo-round. It was made a target to design a system which was fair, uniform and neutral and which meant a further development of the principles laid down in article VII of the GATT in 1947.

To create a fair system thinking was concentrated on one which was based on trade practice and which should aim especially at excluding arbitrary and protectionist practices.

The uniformity was meant to enable the exporter to know exactly what value would be used in the importing country for the calculation of the amount of import duties. This is clearly no less important to the importer.

Finally, the neutrality should prevent the abuse of customs valuation by combating anti-dumping or by supplying artificial protection.

The negotiations finally produced a new customs valuation code. The EEC and the US have applied this code since the first of July 1980, other countries introduced it on the first of January 1981 and in the near future many more countries will follow.

With these developments in mind it is more or less essential that importers and exporters should know of this system. We have not only treated the background and the content of the new system in this book, but some information is also given on other systems of customs valuation.

In conclusion a word on the terminology used. In the following chapters repeated mention is made of the 'General Agreement on Tariffs and Trade' of 1947, and of the 'Agreement on Implementation of Article VII of the General Agreement on Tariffs and Trade' in which the new system of valuation is set out. To avoid confusion we will refer to the former agreement as GATT and to the latter as 'GATT-Code', 'Code for the customs valuation' or (most often) as 'Code'.

Chapter 2. Development of the concept of value

A. AD VALOREM DUTIES AND SPECIFIC DUTIES

A choice is possible between two separate standards on the basis of which taxes levied on importation may be calculated.

One can levy a percentage of the value of the goods on importation (ad valorem duties), or a fixed sum related to physical aspects such as weight or volume (specific duties). Many arguments may be found for or against both possibilities.

It can be said in favour of a specific standard that first and foremost it is simple to apply and its susceptibility to fraud is low. It will usually be easier to establish a products weight than its value, while false declaration of value will be less noticeable than a false declaration of weight.

However, an international preference for ad valorem standards may be seen, especially since the second World War. This is mainly for the following three reasons.

In the first place, its 'social nature'. By choosing the value of the goods as a standard, one is able to respect differences in quality. A tax burden of e.g. 3% of the value, results in a lower duty on low quality, cheap goods than on high quality, expensive goods. This is in contract to specific duties which impose the same burden on similar products, neglecting their differences in quality and price. A specific duty of $ 1 per liter lays the same amount of tax on a bottle of wine costing $ 2 as on a bottle costing $ 60. For the cheap wine this results in a burden of 50%, but the rather more expensive wine (usually bought by the more wealthy) is only burdened with 1,66%.

An ad valorem duty of, say, 10% would in this case result in a tax of $ 0,20 and $ 6 respectively, which does more justice to the 'bearing-power' principle.

In the second place, ad valorem duties automatically follow monetary- and price fluctuations. Considering the high international inflation and the rising prices this may be called an important advantage. Specific rights, on the other hand, would need constant adjustments to get the same result, causing special problems in international agreements in which import duties have been consolidated at certain levels.

Finally, ad valorem duties offer a good point of departure for international tariff-negotiations, as long as the terminology and concepts used are uniform.

The use of this standard, however, brings with it the problem of how to define the concept of value. This problem should not be underestimated.

B. NOTIONAL CONCEPTS AND POSITIVE CONCEPTS

Value is often defined in dictionaries as 'the power of a commodity to purchase others'[1] or in similar terms. Of old, one usually tried to link up to the 'true value of goods in trade'.

The conversion of this apparently concise notion into a workable legal concept has given rise to a lot of discussion, which boils down to two lines of approach, namely the 'notional' and the 'positive'.

A positive concept bases itself on the price actually paid for the goods, or, if for any reason there is no price, on the price paid for comparable goods.

Nevertheless, some people are of the opinion that it is hardly possible to apply a positive concept. They believe the complications, caused by the need to take into account economic and commercial reality correctly in order to guarantee just and equal taxation, can not be overcome. For this reason, they prefer a notional concept, which may be described as 'the price for which the goods could be sold, if they were sold under the conditions of free competition'. This enables one to find the customs value under all circumstances, even if the goods have not been sold but have been delivered free of charge.

C. INTERNATIONAL DEVELOPMENTS

The need for a uniform valuation system was felt before 1940, but during and after the second World War a number of developments occurred in the field of international relations which exerted great influence.

A conference on trade and employment was organised in Havanna under the auspices of the Economic and Social Committee of the United Nations. The results were set out in a charter, which amongst other things gave guide-lines for customs valuation. True results failed to materialize mainly because the US did not bring the charter before the Congress for ratification. As an interim

1. The Concise Oxford Dictionary.

solution the 'General Agreement on Tariffs and Trade' (GATT) was drawn up in London, provisionally coming into effect on 1-1-1948, in which the essence of the Havana charter concerning customs valuation was included (article VII).

In the meantime the 'Study-group for a European Customs Union' was established in Paris, with the drafting of a communal definition of value as one of its aims. The group took article VII of the GATT (see also chapter 5 and annex 1) as a starting-point for its work. The directives laid down in this article see to a system in which:

a. the amount of tax payable shall be certain;

b. international uniformity is necessary to avoid diversion of trade routes for purely fiscal reasons;

c. the value shall be based on the true value, which is taken to mean:
'The price at which at a determined time and place and in the ordinary course of trade such or like merchandise is sold or offered for sale under fully competitive conditions'.

The group's efforts resulted in the 'Convention of the Valuation of Goods for Customs Purposes', concluded in Brussels in 1950.

According to the system set out in this convention, commonly known as the 'Brussels Definition of Value' (BDV), the value was taken to be the 'normal price', defined as:

'The price which the goods would fetch at the time when the duty becomes payable on a sale in the open market between a buyer and a seller independent of each other'.

This system was in use in the EEC up to the first of July 1980, at which time the Code was adopted. In practice the price actually paid (invoice price) was accepted as a basis for the calculation. If necessary an addition was made on account of the buyers secondary undertakings on behalf of the seller or other elements of the value not expressed in the invoice price.

Chapter 3. Background of the Code

The final session of the 'Tokyo-round' was officially held in Geneva in April 1979. This ended a five-year period of intensive negotiations on a variety of tariff and non tariff barriers in international trade.

The multilateral trade negotiations were called the Tokyo-round because the decision to enter upon them was taken in Tokyo in 1973 by 103 countries from all over the world. The convention in Tokyo was the result of initiatives taken by the US, the EEC and Japan, who had already in 1972 agreed to look for new ways of lessening international trade barriers. After the convention in Tokyo, the mechanism of negotiations was established in Geneva, where the actual negotiations took place.

The aim regarding customs value was to arrive at a fair, uniform and neutral system which would be internationally applicable as far as possible. This was needed because it was noted that the principles relating to customs value set out in article VII of the GATT of 1947 did not contain all the elements necessary for an internationally uniform valuation for custons purposes. Moreover, the Brussels definition of value – which developed from these principles – had not been commonly accepted and was not applied by some important countries in international trade (e.g. the US and Canada). Besides, the Brussels definition of value had several disadvantages, of which the following may be mentioned:

a. the definition offered no solution for trade relations between multinationals; this was all the more cogent, as a large volume of international trade (most estimates are between 50 and 70%) passes between international companies;

b. certain elements of the definition were open to quite divergent interpretations (further, chapter 15).

It is naturally simple to say a new definition is needed when one is at the end of negotiations, and to substantiate this in the above manner. It is equally natural that things were not that clear at the start of negotiations.

The Brussels definition of value was being applied by the EEC-member states and several others and had in many cases developed there into a logical system. There were problems, but these will be present in almost any system. The biggest problem was that only 33 nations officially applied the Brussels definition (plus about 65 nations which applied it in fact) while important trading partners abstained. With this situation in mind, and in view of her exports, the EEC tried at the beginning of the negotiations to have the Brussels definition of value accepted (subject to some alterations) as a 'world-wide' system for customs valuation.

Here it should be noted that the EEC-exports to some countries were confronted by more or less aggressive systems of customs valuation, which were so far removed from reality as to be harmful to export. We will mention here the minimum price-system used in several countries and the unpopular American Selling Price in the US.

When the initial strategy came to nought, the EEC followed another course. She produced a draft which not only contained important elements of the American system but also part of its terminology.

The prolonged, and often tough, negotiations took place mostly between the EEC and the US, with Japan, Norway, Sweden, Finland (these last three united in the Nordic block) and the developing nations (mostly represented by India, Argentina and Brazil) clearly taking the second place.

The negotiations finally led to the new Code.

This Code clearly has the character of a compromise. It contains elements (e.g. the computed value, a customs value based on cost, and the inquiry in the exporting country) which the EEC would rather have left out; on the other hand other countries have had to follow the EEC on several points.

The question as to whether the new Code is better or worse than the Brussels definition of value cannot be answered with a simple yes or no. We will merely remark that in our opinion the new Code corresponds more closely with trade practice and leaves less room for all sorts of dogmatic hair-splitting. Those who were able to derive more satisfaction from the problem of value than from a good meal will probably be less happy. However, for trade it means the customs value applied in the importing country is better and more widely known than before, as the transaction value is in most cases accepted as the customs value (subject to minor corrections). A detailed regulation of alternative possibilities exists for cases in which the transaction value is not accepted as the customs value. Provided the new Code is applied by many GATT-partners, the exporters will know their position fairly exactly. Obviously they will also need to know the rate of duty payable, but for this information many authorities are available.

Chapter 4. The developing countries and the Protocol to the Agreement

During the negotiations the developing countries repeatedly voiced their discontent with the Code as it slowly but clearly took shape. Both India and some South-American nations presented several proposals and counter-proposals. The most important objections of the developing countries were:

a. the Code is too complicated and therefore difficult to apply;

b. insufficient power is given to the customs administration, increasing the risk of fraud;

c. the new system causes too large a reduction of the proceeds of import duties, which in many developing nations are the most important source of revenue;

d. the possibility of working with minimum values, set by the state should be left open in order to prevent fraud;

e. the so-called computed value (customs value by calculation of costs) cannot, or can hardly, be applied by developing countries.

These, and other, objections were put forward. However, most of the requests and proposals made by the developing countries contradicted the purpose of the negotiations, namely, to find a fair system offering as few ways of practising veiled protectionism as possible to the countries applying it.

As a result of these objections an article (article 21) was included in the Code, enabling the developing countries to:

a. have a five-year delay in the application of the provisions of the Code, while otherwise enjoying its advantages;

b. postpone the application of certain articles of the Code for a maximum of three years from the actual entry into force;

c. make a request for technical assistance.

The countries in question did not, however, consider this to be sufficient. This controversy finally even resulted in two codes on the valuation of goods for customs purposes being put forward for acceptance during the final session of the negotiations. One of these had been drawn up by the developed countries (the present Code), the other was an alternative drawn up by the developing nations in which the objections already mentioned were met. Clearly this was an unsatisfactory situation. As a result, intensive negotiations between both parties after the actual negotiations had already been concluded led to the drawing up of the 'Protocol to the agreement on implementation of article VII of the General Agreement On Tariffs and Trade'. This protocol, included in this book as annex 4, meets the objections brought forward by the developing countries.

In the first place, they were offered the possibility of postponing the application of the regulations of the agreement for more than five years (a five-year period is already included in the Code). In the second place they are permitted to uphold the use of minimum values to a limited extent during a transition period and to diverge, under certain conditions and/or for a certain period, from other defined points of the Code.

Obviously, the protocol is in fact a serious infraction of the Code's aims. Nevertheless, the price is not too high if it causes a large number of developing nations to acceed to the Code. The desired uniformity of customs valuation will then be attained, albeit a little later.

Chapter 5. The status of the Code and the inclusion in national legislation

A. THE STATUS OF THE CODE

Article VII of the GATT in particular is further developed in the Code. This article (included as annex 1) contains, among others, the following principles for customs valuation:

a. fixed bases and methods should be applied, while being made known in a sufficiently wide circle in order to enable traders to estimate the value to be declared with a reasonable degree of certainty;

b. the value for customs purposes should be based on the actual value of the merchandise on which duty is assessed or of like merchandise;

c. 'actual value' should be taken to be the price at which the imported merchandise or like merchandise is sold or offered for sale in the ordinary course of trade under fully competitive conditions;

d. if no actual value is available, customs value should be based on the nearest equivalent of such value;

e. the value for customs purposes may not be based on the value of merchandise of national origin or on arbitrary or fictitious values;

f. foreign currency should be converted into national currency in accordance with internationally agreed exchange rates. If no such rates are available the conversion rate should effectively reflect the current value of such currency.

Naturally, these principles do not form a complete system of valuation of goods. In actual fact these provisions were formulated with such lack of precision that the GATT-partners were left too much room for their own practices, frustrating uniform application. This is one of the reasons which led to the new Code on the valuation of goods for customs purposes.

The Code is not directly applicable. The Code's provisions must first be included in national -, and in the case of the EEC-members, community legislation. This has certain risks. On the conversion into national law, a country could dilute the Code with a measure of national philosophy on value, thus losing the desired uniformity.

This risk is reduced by the inclusion into the Code of a very large number of precisely formulated provisions (and by being rather more detailed than article VII of the GATT and the Brussels definition of value). In this context mention should also be made of part II of the Code, which concerns the administration of the agreement and the settlement of disputes. A number of international measures are supplied therein in order to ensure an internationally uniform application of the Code. In this we see another fundamental difference from the Brussels definition of value. We will come back to this part of the Code further on (chapter 7).

B. INCLUSION IN NATIONAL LEGISLATION

We have noted earlier that the provisions of the Code must be included in the national legislation (community legislation in the EEC) of the countries applying the Code. As the articles on the system of valuation are extremely detailed they will obviously be included in national legislation almost literally. This has for instance been the case in the US and also in the EEC albeit the EEC has unfortunately numbered the articles differently.

By copying the provisions literally whenever possible one avoids complaints from other nations that the Code has not been applied correctly, while also minimising the risk of different interpretations. Obviously an exporter will not always be able to avoid studying the legislation of a foreign country, but this study will probably be concentrated on e.g. the procedure of appeal or on the declaration-procedure rather than on the system of customs valuation itself.

Regarding EEC-legislation, its framework is as follows:

a. A basic regulation, enacted by the Council of Ministers[1] establishes the rules of valuation in conformity with the provisions of the GATT-code and delegates the competency for further legislation to the Commission of the EEC. A committee, established by this regulation and consisting of representatives of the member-states with a representative of the Commission as chairman, shall advise the Commission. This committee shall also examine questions concerning the application of the new system.

b. A number of Commission-regulations, of which the following are already enacted:

1. a basic regulation implementing certain provisions of the council regulation;[2]

1. Regulation (EEC) 1224/80 of the Council, 28-5-1980; OJ No. L 134.
2. Regulation (EEC) 1495/80 of the Commission, 11-6-1980; OJ No. L 154.

2. a regulation on the interpretative notes and generally accepted accounting principles;[1]
3. a regulation concerning the declaration of particulars relating to customs value;[2]
4. a regulation extending, as a transitional measure, the validity of certain regulations based on the BDV;[3]
5. a number of regulations concerning costs of transport, the place of entry and postal charges.[4]

1. Regulation (EEC) 1494/80 of the Commission, 11-6-1980; OJ No. L 154.
2. Regulation (EEC) 1496/80 of the Commission, 11-6-1980; OJ No. L 154.
3. Regulation (EEC) 1493/80 of the Commission, 11-6-1980; OJ No. L 154.
4. Regulations (EEC) 3177/80 – 3179/80 of the Commission, 12-2-1980; OJ No. L. 335.

Chapter 6. Structure of the Code

A. THE ARTICLES OF THE CODE

The articles of the Code can be divided into two groups, namely articles relating to the new customs valuation system, and articles on other subjects.

1. The new customs valuation system

The primary basis of the new system is, as is stated in the Code's introductory commentary, the acknowledgement that whenever possible the transaction value should be taken as the basis for the calculation of customs value.

As a positive definition starts from the price paid, a further differentiation is needed when there has been no sale (lease, transfer within the company, hire etc.).

The Code contains a total of 6 different methods (articles 1 up to and including 7) in a hierachical relationship to each other:
1. the transaction value of the imported goods (art. 1);
2. the transaction value of identical goods (art. 2);
3. the transaction value of similar goods (art. 3);
4. the deductive value (art. 5);
5. the computed value (art. 6);
6. the flexible valuation method (art. 7).

Only if the customs value cannot be determined under the provisions of the first method, starting with method number 1, the next methods may be tried. An exception to this rule is formed by the importers right to request the order of application of methods 4 and 5 be reversed (art. 4).

The 6 methods enumerated above are treated in chapter 8 to 13, one chapter being devoted to each method. In article 8 of the Code several criteria are enumerated for raising (and sometimes lowering) the price paid or payable for the merchandise if such criteria are not already expressed in the price. This article is treated together with the first method (the transaction value of the imported goods) in chapter 8.

2. The remaining articles

Besides the valuation system, the Code regulates a number of subjects falling outside the scope of this work. We will glance at the most important of these. These provisions are directed towards prevention of incorrect customs valuation practice, the achievement of maximum uniformity and providing importers with the necessary legal security. Thus article 9 stipulates that the conversion of currency should take place according to duly published exchange rates which reflect as effectively as possible the current value of the currency.

Article 11 contains a provision for the settlement of disputes. It is stated therein that any person liable for the payment of duty should have the right of appeal, without penalty. The initial appeal may be made to an authority within the customs administration, but it should be possible to make a final appeal to a judicial authority.

Another of the importers rights is laid down in article 13. If for any reason the final determination of the customs value is to be delayed, the importer is allowed to withdraw the goods from customs if he provides sufficient guarantee covering the ultimate payment of customs duties.

Article 16 also watches over the importers interests and attempts to combat arbitrary customs valuation. It requires the customs to inform the interested party, in writing and on demand, as to how the customs value of the imported goods was determined.

Secrecy is enjoined upon the customs administration by article 10, which provides that no information which is by nature confidential or which is provided on a confidential basis shall be disclosed by the authorities without the specific permission of the parties concerned. Apparently the claim that laws, regulations and administrative rulings of general application should be properly published and proclaimed is not generally accepted. At least, article 12 contains a provision charging the contracting states to publish laws, decisions and rulings giving effect to the Code.

A number of articles is devoted to the administration of the Code and settlement of dispute between countries. We will come back to these subjects in chapter 7.

Finally there are several articles dealing with acceptance and accession, entry into force and other matters of little or no concern to the importer or exporter.

B. THE ANNEXES

The Code is followed by three annexes. In fact, only annex I is of interest to traders. It contains a commentary, the 'interpretative notes'. This commentary (article by article) forms an integral part of the agreement, thus having the same force, so that countries which have accepted the Code are bound equally by the articles and the commentary. These interpretative notes have been consulted in the preparation of this book whenever necessary.

The Code's annexes II and III deal with respectively the technical committee on customs valuation and the ad hoc panels. These subjects are discussed indirectly in chapter 7.

Chapter 7. Administration of the Code and dispute settlement

The Code pays extensive attention to the administration of the agreement and to consultation in case of a difference of opinion. Also included is a procedure for the settlement of dispute. Two committees have been instituted for the purpose of administration. The one we would like to call the trade-political committee (officially 'the Committee on Customs Valuation') and the other the committee of customs experts (officially 'the Technical Committee on Customs Valuation').

The trade-political committee is made up out of representatives of the parties to the agreement and meets in principle once a year in Geneva. It makes use of the GATT secretariat. This committee especially concerns itself with the way in which the Code is applied by the parties and also has certain duties when a dispute concerning the application of the Code has arisen between parties.

The countries concerned will usually first consult each other when a dispute exists. A country will do this whenever it considers the valuation practice in another country to be contrary to the principles of the Code to such an extent as to bring serious harm to its own trade interests.

The parties can ask the Technical Committee for advice and assistance.

The trade-political committee shall meet as soon as possible at the request of one of the parties concerned, if consultations between the parties do not lead to a satisfactory result, in order to find a solution. For this, several instruments are available to this committee. The Technical Committee can be requested to carry out an examination if the problem is of a technical nature or a panel may be instituted if the conflict has a trade-political background.

It would go too far to elaborate the working method of the Technical Committee and the panels and the way in which disputes may be settled. In the end the procedure (unless the dispute is settled before) results in a recommendation by the Committee on Customs Valuation made to one or more of the parties concerned, or in another decision considered necessary by this committee.

When this procedure has been followed and no solution has been found, the parties have recourse to the provisions of the GATT, especially the articles XXII and XXIII. These articles supply the following consecutive measures: consultations at different levels, an inquiry by the joint GATT-members and steps against the country concerned if necessary (for instance, withdrawal of concessions).

It is important to exporters to have a broad knowledge of the above. If an exporter thinks the customs valuation practice in a certain country contrary to the Code, resulting in his having to pay more duties than were to be expected from the available data, he can turn to his own administration with as many facts as possible. If these authorities share his opinion, they can institute the proceedings described above against the country concerned.

And finally a word on the Technical Committee on Customs Valuation: this committee is made up out of representatives of the parties and meets at least twice a year in Brussels. It makes use of the secretariat of the Customs Cooperation Council.[1] As the name implies, it is concerned with technical aspects of the customs valuation, it provides the parties with information and advice and gives technical assistance (probably especially to developing nations). Furthermore, it is hoped that this committee will draw up Explanatory Notes to the Code, thus ensuring an internationally uniform application.

1. Established by the Convention of 15-12-1950, which is accepted by 87 countries including the EEC and the US. The Council is required to make recommendations to ensure uniform interpretation of the Conventions of Nomenclature and Valuation (BDV) and has a general responsability to secure harmony and uniformity in customs systems.

Chapter 8. The transaction value of the imported goods

SURVEY

The customs value according to the first method is the transaction value. That is to say, the price actually paid or payable for the goods when sold for export to the country of importation (article 1), which is raised or lowered according to a number of provisions found in article 8, and subject to the proviso that a number of conditions (set out in article 1) are met.

Because of the amount of material to be discussed, we have split this chapter into three sub-chapters:

I. Elements of the transaction value

In this sub-chapter we wil discuss the three elements which may be found in the description of the transaction value, to wit:

A. Price actually paid or payable.
B. For the goods.
C. Sold for export to the country of importation.

II. Adjustment of the price paid or payable

The price actually paid or payable shall be adjusted with relation to:

A. Elements chargeable to the buyer which are not included in the price paid or payable (commissions, cost of packing etc.).
B. Activities considered as indirect payment (e.g. materials or services supplied by the buyer).
C. Royalties and licence fees, and shares in the proceeds of subsequent sale.
D. Cost associated with the transport.
E. Elements not forming part of the customs value.

III. Conditions to be met

The transaction value has to fullfill certain conditions. They see to:

A. Restrictions as to the use of the goods by the buyer.
B. Conditions or considerations for which no value can be determined.

C. The proceeds of any subsequent resale or use of the goods by the buyer accruing to the seller.
D. A possible relationship between buyer and seller.

I. ELEMENTS OF THE TRANSACTION VALUE

A. THE PRICE ACTUALLY PAID OR PAYABLE

1. The price

The price actually paid or payable is the total payment made or to be made by the buyer to, or for the benefit of, the seller in accordance with the conditions of the contract of sale. The payment is not necessarily made by the transfer of money, but may also be made by way of letters of credit or negotiable instruments etc.

The acting in accordance with the conditions of the contract of sale is decisive, i.e. the payment must be related to the imported merchandise.

2. Method of payment

Payment may be made directly or indirectly. As an example of the latter, a payment may be made by the buyer to a third party in order to settle a debt the seller owes to this third party. If the buyer acts in accordance with obligations in the contract of sale, then these payments are included in the price actually paid and therefore included in the customs value.

A number of activities which are enumerated in article 8 of the Code (below, under II B) are considered to be indirect payment and will result in an addition if they are undertaken by the buyer and are not included in the price paid or payable.

This is an exhaustive enumeration. Activities not listed are not considered to be indirect payments, even if they are performed by the buyer to the profit of the seller.

In this context it is important to consider the provision on activities relating to the marketing of the goods undertaken by the buyer on his own account. These include marketing, advertising and warranty. Such activities are not considered as being indirect payment. This is not even the case if they are to the advantage of the seller, or even if they are undertaken by agreement with the seller.

It should, however, be noted that these costs are a part of the transaction value for which no deduction is to be made when calculating the customs value whenever the seller pays them himself, includes them in the price or invoices them seperately.

3. Possible discounts

The Code considers each importation as a seperate case, for which normal practice is no longer decisive. Whatever the buyer and seller have agreed for a specific case is respected, though naturally subject to the fixed conditions. The size and normality of a reduction in price, given on account of cash payment or buying in bulk etc. will therefore be of no importance.

Discounts are not mentioned in the Code, which restricts itself to the price paid or payable. When buyer and seller have agreed on a certain price, which has been paid before the declaration is made, that 'price actually paid' is taken as the customs value. Whether this price has been found by raising or by lowering a basic price is of no consequence.

It is our belief that if, when the price has not yet been paid on the moment that the customs value is to be determined, the importer claims a stated discount on the amount invoiced, such a claim should be honoured if two conditions are met:

a. the discount should be related to the imported merchandise,
b. the discount should be definitely fixed at the moment of declaration.

It is generally accepted, both in the US and the EEC, that a discount for cash payment (e.g. a 2% discount on payment within 7 days, 1% on payment within 14 days, invoice dated July 1) is definite at the moment of declaration. The customs administration is free, however to ask for additional information. We believe that if, in the example given, the declaration is made before the 8th of July the price payable should be taken to be 98% of the invoice amount. In other cases (e.g. quantity discounts) it should be strictly maintained the discount should be fixed when the declaration is made.

If, for example, the manufacturer offers a discount for quantities of more than 1000 units bought within one year this should be taken into account for the customs valuation only when the amount of the invoice is actually decreased on the importation of unit 1001.

B. FOR THE GOODS

1. General

The Code's positive approach takes the price paid for the goods actually imported, irrespective of the total quantity covered by the contract of sale in question. If the imported goods are part of a larger consignment, bought as a whole but most of which has followed another destination, the customs value may be found by taking a part of the transaction value proportional to the value of the complete consignment.

Example:
a. Sale of 10,000 units at $ 2, price $ 20,000.
b. 3,000 units imported into a country using the Code, the remaining 7,000 units are not imported.
The customs value of this consignment (3/10 of the total) is 3/10 of the price actually paid ($ 20,000) i.e. $ 6,000.

No account is taken of the fact that the price of the complete consignment is usually relatively lower than the price of a part of the consignment.

2. Damaged goods, shipments with shortages

The customs value is the price actually paid or payable for the imported goods.

This means the customs administration has to find the price actually paid or payable for the amount of merchandise declared.

In cases where goods have been damaged during transport or when only part of the shipment reaches its destination (part of it having been lost etc.) it should in our opinion be assumed that unless a new price has been agreed which may be taken as the transaction value:
a. the amount invoiced does not represent the actual value;
b. the transaction value method is not applicable;
c. the customs value therefore has to be established according to one of the other methods.

C. SOLD FOR EXPORT TO THE COUNTRY OF IMPORTATION

Sale of the goods is a basic condition for the applicability of method 1. The question which agreements may be taken as a contract of sale remains unanswered in the Code. We believe two basic conditions are involved.

The contract of sale shall have to obligate the seller to transfer ownership, against which the buyer shall have the obligation to pay a price.

In practice a reference should be made to civil law. To our opinion this condition in the Code is met when there is a legal contract of sale (shown for instance by a written contract between parties).

It is of no consequence where the buyer is established. This may be inside or outside the country into which the goods are imported.

The place where the agreement is made is equally unimportant. We would state that this place may be the international market as well as (under certain conditions) the market of the exporting country. Consider in this context the entrepreneur who buys machine parts on the market of the exporting country and imports them himself, or the tourists who declare the souvenirs purchased abroad.

The second condition in the Code states there should be a sale made 'for export to the country of importation', a condition which is not very clear.

There are no problems with goods sold by an American exporter to a Dutch importer, which are immediately shipped directly from New York to Rotterdam. However, other situations can give rise to discussion. To avoid serious problems, e.g. when the destination of goods is changed repeatedly during transport or when they are sold 'en route', a standard has been fixed within the EEC which offers a pragmatic solution for such cases.[1] The fact that the goods are declared and imported suffices for the assumption they have been sold for export. As a result, when the goods are declared, the customs administration is not concerned with the question whether or not the intent to import the goods into the ultimate country of destination existed at the time the contract of sale was concluded.

It is not yet known what views other countries hold on this matter.

Nevertheless, one has to keep in mind this does not answer the question which transaction value is acceptable if the goods have been sold several times before importation.

It may be assumed the condition 'sold for export' has been met when the goods are eventually imported into the EEC after four consecutive transactions.

Which of the four transactions provides the transaction value is quite a different problem.

Example 1

A consignment of cocoa-beans is on its way from South-America to Europe. The owner is A, who has bought them in the country of origin.

A – – – – – B – – – – – C

1. Regulation (EEC) 1495/80, article 6; OJ No. L 154.

The consignment is sold at sea to B, who resells it to C. C imports the goods. It is of no consequence if the intent to import the goods existed at the time of purchase. A declaration of importation suffices. The transaction value is the price B–C.

Example 2

B (Norway) buys from A (Japan). B sells to the Dutch importer C. The goods are sent directly to C by A. C declares the goods.

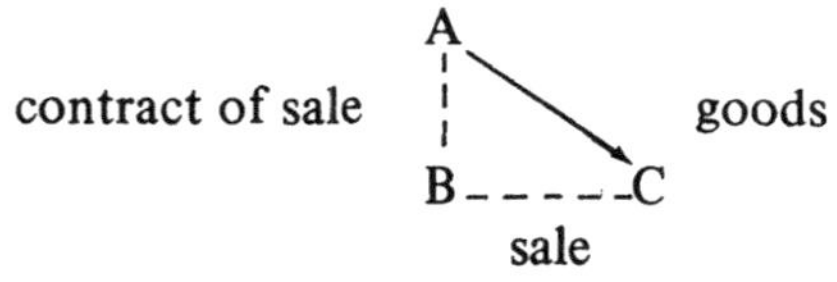

This declaration demonstrates the condition of 'sold for export' has been met in spite of the fact the importation is the result of a transaction Japan-Norway. The price B–C can be taken as the transaction value.

However, the question may arise whether the price A–B can be taken as the transaction value when C declares the goods. It is clearly unlikely B will inform C of the price he has had to pay A.

If, however, this were to be the case, the question has in our opinion to be answered in the affirmative. This is the case because the condition that the goods should be sold has been met. As they have been imported it can also be assumed they have been sold for export. If the declarant is able to supply the customs administration with the necessary documentation and information nothing prevents that particular transaction value being accepted.

Since the discussion concerning this point has not yet been concluded it is uncertain if this will become the official view. Seeing the viewpoint of the EEC in this matter such an expectation to our opinion appears justified.

II. ADJUSTMENT OF THE PRICE PAID OR PAYABLE

GENERAL

An adjustment of the price actually paid or payable is provided by the Code for a number of cases in which the customs value is found by the use of method 1. To this end two general conditions for additions are set out in article 8:

a. an addition may only be made on the basis of objective and quantifiable data. A rather vague criterion, inspired by the wish to put an end to arbitrary decisions. An addition may only be made if a calculation can be shown to be correctly made;

b. no additions other than those mentioned in article 8 are allowed.

In this sub-chapter the following will be treated consecutively:

A. Elements chargeable to the buyer

The price paid or payable is increased by a number of elements whenever they are chargeable to the buyer and not included in the price, to wit:
1. commissions and brokerage;
2. cost of containers and cost of packing.

B. Activities considered to be indirect payment

Under certain circumstances goods supplied and services rendered by the buyer are regarded as indirect payment. The following are concerned:
1. materials, components and the like;
2. tools, dies, moulds and similar items;
3. engineering, development, design work, plans etc.

C. Royalties and benefit of subsequent resale

Apart from paying the price, a buyer sometimes pays royalties for the imported goods or gives the seller part of the proceeds of the subsequent use or resale. In such a case the price paid or payable is raised with that amount of money.

D. Cost associated with the transport

Each contracting Party (to the Code) may choose whether or not to include these costs in the customs value.

E. Elements not forming part of the customs value

The transaction value may include a number of elements which are definitely not meant to be included in the customs value. These may be deducted.

A. ELEMENTS CHARGEABLE TO THE BUYER

1. Commissions and brokerage

The services of an intermediary, who has negotiated the contract of sale on behalf of the seller, will generally be charged to the seller and subsequently be included in the price.

On the other hand, the transaction value is increased with this sum to find the customs value if these costs are paid directly by the buyer, separate from the price.

Buying commissions, by which the Code means the payment made by an importer to his agent for representation at the purchase abroad, are explicitly excluded from the customs value.

2. Cost of containers and cost of packing

Containers will often be used several times. In such cases the costs may either be apportioned to the different consignments or charged as a whole to one consignment. However, the amount charged for containers is included in the customs value when they can only be used once and their costs are not included in the price.

Regarding the cost of packing, these are taken to be part of the price of the goods. If this is not the case and these costs are still charged to the buyer they are to be added to the transaction value in order to find the customs value.

B. ACTIVITIES CONSIDERED TO BE INDIRECT PAYMENT

Only a limited group of goods and services is involved, while a number of factors must be taken into account.

a. the buyer supplies goods or services free of charge or at a reduced cost;
b. for use in connection with the production and sale;
c. an addition is only made to the extent that the value is not included in the price.

If any occur, the element concerned should be apportioned in a reasonable manner appropriate to the circumstances and in accordance with generally accepted accounting principles.

1. Materials, components etc. incorporated in the imported goods and materials consumed in their production

As opposed to materials incorporated in the goods (actually present in the imported goods) the second category relates to materials of which no remains are found in the imported goods after their use. These may for instance be chemicals used to speed up a certain reaction.

2. Tools, dies, moulds and similar items

As to the value to be added on account of tools, moulds etc. supplied by the importer a distinction should be made between the case in which the importer or a person related to him produces the element, and the case in which the importer obtains goods/services from a third party. In the first case the production costs (and not the value in trade) including costs of transport to the place of manufacture are the value. If the goods are obtained from a third party the costs against which the importer obtains them are the value. The value of, say, a die should be apportioned to the imported goods.

Several methods are available, e.g. the value could be added as a whole to a certain shipment, or be apportioned over the entire anticipated production, whichever the importer prefers. This will also depend on the way in which the importer is able to supply data to the customs administration.

3. Engineering, development, design work, plans, etc.

In this category an important part is played by the condition set down in article 8, paragraph 3, namely that additions to the price paid should only be made on the basis of objective and quantifiable data.

To avoid problems, it is stated in the note to article 8 that, whenever possible, use should be made of data found in the buyers documentation on the transaction.

Two general conditions are found in article 8, first paragraph, letter b-IV:

a. The element must have been produced elsewhere than in the country of importation. This is to be interpreted strictly. An addition can not be made whenever the element is produced by anyone within the country of importation.

b. The element must be necessary for the production of the imported goods. This may obviously lead to discussion, but should in our opinion be interpreted in the narrowest sense. The invention of the wheel is not included, nor is the preliminary designwork which comes before the definite design supplied by the buyer.

The value of the element is added. If the buyer has himself bought or leased the element for a certain price, that price is taken to be the value. If the buyer has produced the element himself, the production cost should be considered to be its value. No addition should be made for elements belonging to the public domain, except for possible cost of obtaining copies.

The value is apportioned in the same way as was stated regarding the value of tools, dies, etc. Depending on the data supplied by the importer the value will be spread over the total quantity produced or over an imported quantity.

C. ROYALTIES AND BENEFITS OF SUBSEQUENT RESALE

1. Royalties and licence fees

Whenever the buyer is obliged to pay a royalty or a licence fee in addition to the price of the goods, this payment is included in the customs value. By royalties and licence fees the Code also means the payments made for patents, trademarks, copyrights, etc. However, the charges for the right to reproduce the imported goods should not be added to the price.

Two further conditions are set out in article 8:

a. the royalty must be related to the goods being imported;
b. the payment must be a condition of sale of the goods.

An important part is again played by the objective and quantifiable data, as these conditions do not offer much more than a general pointer. According to the Code a check should be made in each case whether or not the royalty or licence fee is related to the goods. Practice will have to supply the necessary body to this cryptic stipulation. No addition should be made for a royalty when there is only a partial relation, unless an objective calculation can be made.

The stipulation that the payment is to be a condition of sale will apparently not result in an addition being made without any further ado. The fact that a royalty is paid is of no importance by itself. We believe it will have to be checked whether an agreement would have been without a royalty being paid. An important indication may be found in the way the parties have fixed their undertakings in a contract. There is no general standard for finding whether or not something is a condition of sale.

The Code also mentions both direct - and indirect payments are concerned. Therefore, the payment of royalty made by the buyer to a third party may also result in an increase in the transaction value, as long as it is a condition of sale.

2. Benefits of subsequent resale or use of the imported goods

The benefits accrueing to the seller after the sale make up the final group of elements which result in an increase of the transaction value. This concerns any part of the proceeds of any subsequent resale, disposal or use of the goods by the buyer that accrues directly or indirectly to the seller.

It is very important indeed to make a clear distinction between this stipulation and the previous one. It has definitely not been the purpose to consider a payment of royalty, which has not led to an increase in the transaction value under the provisions of article 8, paragraph 1, because it was no condition of sale, as a benefit accrueing to the seller resulting in an addition under article 8, paragraph 1d. Whenever such a payment has not resulted in an addition under the provisions of article 8, paragraph 1c, it is not taken into further consideration.

D. COST ASSOCIATED WITH THE TRANSPORT

Apart from elements related to the production and sale of the goods, which always result in an addition being made, the Code also refers to several elements which are connected with transport. With regard to this category each Party to the Agreement has been left the choice whether or not to include these costs in the customs value by means of national legislation. This is because of the difference concerning the basis of valuation existing between the US and the EEC as well as a large number of other nations at the time the Code was completed. The US based, and still base themselves on f.o.b.[1] -conditions while others use a c.i.f.[2] -price up to their national borders.

The cost of transport, loading, unloading and handling charges associated with the transport and the cost of insurance are mentioned successively in the Code. Each Party has the choice, as long as costs up to the point of entry are concerned, whether or not to add them to the value.

As for this point, the adoption of the Code has not led to any change. The US uses its f.o.b.-approach, the EEC a c.i.f.-price.

It is stated in the Code that the part of these costs connected with transport within the importing country should not be included in the customs value, provided it is distinguishable.

E. ELEMENTS NOT FORMING PART OF THE CUSTOMS VALUE

The note to article 1 of the Code lists a number of costs which are not included in the value provided that they are distinguished from the price actually paid.

These are:

1. Free on board
2. Cost, insurance, freight

a. charges for construction, erection, assembly, maintenance or technical assistance, undertaken after importation;
b. the cost of transport after importation;
c. duties and taxes of the country of importation.

The condition they should be 'distinguished from the price' may give rise to misunderstanding.

It should be made clear these costs can never lead to an addition if they are *not* included in the price. The additions which may be made are enumerated exhaustively in article 8 and these costs are not included.

The stipulation, therefore, seems superfluous. What is its meaning?

In some cases (delivery free domicile of an assembled machine) the above costs are all included in the price which is taken by the customs administration as the price actually paid.

Import duties should, however, only be levied on the value of the merchandise.

The Code seems to advise invoicing everything separately in order to avoid such problems. In our opinion this may be given a broad interpretation. It is sufficient to be able to distinguish these costs from the price paid (i.e. by means of contracts, invoices, calculations etc.). Where this is the case they may be deducted from the price to establish the customs value.

It is not certain, however, that this liberal view will be held by all countries using the Code. During the negotiations in Geneva a number of countries urged to include an article which would, as a counterpart of article 8, name a few deductible items. Such an article has not been included, which is hardly surprising because of the indefinite character of such elements.

However, it is recommendable to invoice all elements beyond the scope of the transaction value in the sense of article 1 either separately or in such a way that they are distinguishable.

III. CONDITIONS TO BE MET BY THE TRANSACTION VALUE

GENERAL

The transaction value found after making the adjustments according to article 8 must meet four further conditions set out in the Code if this method is to be used:

A. there are to be no restrictions as to the disposition or use of the goods by the buyer;
B. the price may not be subject to a condition or consideration for which a value cannot be determined;

C. no part of the proceeds of any subsequent resale, disposal or use of the goods by the buyer may accrue directly or indirectly to the seller (this is the case, for instance, when A sells goods to B for a price of $ 1 per kg, with the supplementary condition that 50% of the profits on resale will accrue to him);
D. where the buyer and seller are related, the relation may not have had any influence on the price.

Method 1 may not be used for the valuation of goods for customs purposes if anyone of these conditions is not met. These conditions are discussed in greater depth in this sub-chapter.

A. RESTRICTIONS AS TO THE USE OF THE GOODS

The price may not be used as a basis for the customs value if the contract of sale limits the buyer's freedom to use the goods, unless it concerns a limitation which:

a. is imposed or required by law or by the public authorities in the country of importation, or
b. limits the geographical area, or
c. does not substantially affect the value of the goods.

The case in which the seller demands the product should not be put on display prior to a fixed date, is for instance taken as being such an acceptable limitation.

B. CONDITIONS OR CONSIDERATIONS FOR WHICH A VALUE CANNOT BE DETERMINED

The price paid will not be accepted by the customs administration if the sale is made under provisions for which no value can be determined. This is the case, for instance, where the seller charges a certain price provided that the buyer also purchases other products.

This also means that if the value of the condition or undertaking can be determined it will be regarded as an indirect payment resulting in an increase of the price paid. After all, the transaction value covers the total payment, both indirect and direct, made by the buyer to the seller.

Nevertheless, the price paid will not be rejected as a result of any condition or undertaking concerning:

a. production and/or
b. marketing of the goods.

With respect to production, undertakings will be concerned which have not resulted in an addition under the provisions of article 8, e.g. a design produced in the importing country.

The phrase 'relating to the marketing' covers all activities related to marketing, promotion, advertising and warranty. This structure prevents discussions as well as arbitrary decisions. The value of activities listed above will not be included in the customs value even if they are the result of a contract with the seller.

C. PROCEEDS OF ANY SUBSEQUENT RESALE OR USE OF THE GOODS BY THE BUYER THAT ACCRUE TO THE SELLER

This concerns another condition which should be related to article 8. In that article it is stated that the value of the share in the proceeds of resale or later use by the buyer which accrues to the seller, either directly or indirectly, should be included in the customs value.

The transaction value cannot be accepted as the customs value if such a benefit is found and if it can not be added to the price under the provisions of article 8 because its value cannot be determined etc. In such a case the method set out in article 1 cannot be used.

D. RELATIONSHIP BETWEEN THE BUYER AND SELLER

1. Acceptability of the transaction value

The existence of a relationship forms no reason by itself for rejecting the transaction value. It is to be examined whether or not the price has been influenced by the relationship between buyer and seller to an extent that it is not acceptable as a basis for the customs value. As the Code does not, as would be the case with a notional concept, take normal practice as a standard, the question arises when such an 'influencing' is present. To that end, the customs service will have to examine the circumstances surrounding the sale, by means of data supplied by the importer.

Such an examination will not be made in all cases. There will only be an inquiry when the customs administration has doubts. Should this be the case, the examination will include the build-up of the price and all relevant aspects of the transaction, including the way in which the trade-relation is organised by the buyer and seller.

The Code lists several elements which may show the relation has had no influence on the price, and that the buyer and seller act as though unrelated, to wit:

a. the price has been settled in a manner consistent with the normal pricing practices of the industry in question;

b. the price has been settled in consistence with sales to buyers who are not related;

c. the price is sufficient to ensure recovery of all costs plus a profit which is representative of the firms overall profit realised over a representative period of time.

Normative for a positive approach is what is established in a specific case, taking the commercial circumstances into account. It is therefore impossible to look at a profit-margin in the light of what is usual in the line of business concerned. The question is what is typical for this specific business.

2. Test values

Article 1, paragraph 2, letter b, provides a totally new possibility for the related importer to use his transaction value as the customs value.

The transaction value is to be accepted by the customs administration, irrespective of any influence on the price, if the importer shows that value to be very close to one of the following three values:[1]

a. the transaction value in sales to unrelated buyers of identical or similar goods for export to the same country of importation;

b. the customs value of identical or similar goods as determined under the provisions of the deductive value;

c. the customs value of identical or similar goods as determined under the provisions of the computed value.

The value concerned should also have been accepted by the customs administration earlier on. There are some further limitations. The values will have to be found in the same period, while the transaction value will have to approximate the test value closely. The note to article 1 states that to discover if this is the case account should be taken of the nature of the goods, the nature of the industry itself, the season, possible commercial differences etc. The importer's transaction value will have to be accepted as a basis for customs valuation by means of methode 1 if these conditions have been met, irrespective of any influence of the price found.

1. Originally there was a fourth test-value included, which has been deleted by acceptance of the protocol to the Code.

The test values must be used if the importer requests it and can only be used as material for comparison.

They may definitely not be used to establish substitute values. Furthermore, the customs administration cannot demonstrate that there has been an influence on the price if the importer is unable to or refuses to show that the transaction value approximates a test value.

Chapter 9. The transaction value of identical goods

A. DEFINITION

If for any reason method 1 should not be applicable, the customs value will be formed by the transaction value of identical goods, which are:
a. sold for export to the same country of importation and
b. exported at or about the same time as the goods being valued.

By 'identical goods' are meant those goods which are the same in all respects, including physical characteristics, quality and reputation. Minor differences in appearance (e.g. colour) would not preclude goods otherwise conforming to the definition from being regarded as identical.

These goods must have also been:
a. produced in the same country as the goods being valued,
b. produced by the same person.

Reference may only be made to identical goods produced by another manufacturer if no such identical goods produced by the same person exist.

B. ELEMENTS

1. The transaction value

This method is concerned with the transaction value of identical goods, that is to say with a customs value which has been accepted in accordance with method 1 earlier on. It should be noted in this context that goods containing engineering, drawings etc. made in the country of importation (article 8, par. 1, letter b-IV), for which therefore no adjustments have been made, cannot be taken to be identical goods.

2. Same commercial level and quantity

The identical goods must have been sold at the same commercial level and in substantially the same quantity as the goods being valued.

If such a sale cannot be found, a price may be used which was reached at a different commercial level and/or for a different quantity, and which is adjusted in order to take these differences into account. Such an adjustment must be reasonable and realistic. This requires proof, which may for example be supplied by means of bona fide price lists, showing prices for different quantities.

Depending on whether the customs administration of the importing country uses a c.i.f.- or a f.o.b.-approach (chapter 8, sub II.D) the costs mentioned in article 8, paragraph 2, will possibly be included in the transaction value of identical goods. This value will then perhaps have to be adjusted to take differences in the method of transportation etc. into account.

If several transaction values of identical goods are available, the lowest will be used to establish the value of the imported goods.

3. Exported at or about the same time

The identical goods should have been sold for export to the same country of importation, but they need not have been sold at the same time as the goods being valued.

Furthermore, they need not be imported at the same time. The only condition is that the identical goods have been exported at or about the same time.

It is not clear when can be spoken of 'about the same time'. A lot will depend on the stability of prices in a certain line of business. This concept can be given a broad interpretation where prices are stable. However, if prices fluctuate considerably a narrow interpretation seems more appropriate (as a comparison, the Dutch customs administration interprets 'about the same time' as not more than two months before or after the day of export).

Chapter 10. The transaction value of similar goods

A. DEFINITION

This method of valuation is nearly the same as the previous method. The difference is that in this case the transaction value of similar goods is taken as the customs value.

Similar goods means goods which, although not alike in all respects, have like characteristics and like component materials which enable them to perform the same functions and to be commercially interchangeable. The quality of the goods, their reputation and the existence of a trademark are among the factors to be considered. Regarding the similarity of goods of different trademarks, it will especially be necessary to consider the commercial interchangeability.

B. ELEMENTS

For the discussion of the different elements of this method we refer the reader to what has been stated concerning method number 2, the transaction value of identical goods (chapter 9).

Chapter 11. The deductive value

A. REVERSAL OF THE ORDER OF APPLICATION OF METHODS 4 AND 5

If the customs value cannot be determined by means of the first three methods, the importer may show preference for the application of the fifth method before the fourth method (see art. 4 Code).

The developing countries have been given the opportunity (Protocol to the Code, article 1, paragraph 4) to provide that such a choice will need the approval of the customs authorities.

B. THE METHOD

The starting-point for the deductive value is the price for which the imported goods or identical or similar imported goods are sold in the country of importation to persons who are unrelated to the sellers of the goods.

The customs value is then found by deducting a certain number of costs incurred after importation together with the usual margin of profit or commission from this price.

The deductible amount should whenever possible be based on data supplied by or on behalf of the importer.

Article 5 covers three situations, depending on whether the goods:

a. are sold in the condition as imported at or about the time of importation;
b. are sold after some time has passed, or
c. are sold after further processing.

This method does not include a special order of application of prices of imported, identical or similar goods. That is to say it is unnecessary to wait for another sale of imported or identical goods if there is a sale of similar imported goods at the time of importation.

C. SALE AT OR ABOUT THE TIME OF IMPORTATION

First of all it should be remarked that the price actually paid for the imported goods is irrelevant.

The price at which the goods are resold at or about the time of importation is taken as a starting-point, irrespective of any, possibly large, changes in price which may have taken place between the time of importation and the time at which the importer acquired the goods.

The concept 'at or about the time of importation' will again be interpreted broadly or strictly, depending on the stability of prices.

The price per unit for which the goods are sold to unrelated buyers in the greatest aggregate quantity is decisive. This concept is defined in the Code as being the price at which the greatest number of units is sold at the first commercial level after importation.

Example

quantity sold	price per unit
60 units	110
35 units	95
40 units	100
20 units	90
70 units	105
40 units	95

The price at which the greatest number of units is sold is 95 (i.e. 35 + 40 units). The price per unit sold in the greatest aggregate quantity is therefore 95.

A sale to someone who has supplied goods or services used for the production or sale for export of the goods imported (as referred to in article 8, paragraph 1, letter b), free of charge or for a reduced price cannot be taken into account for the application of this method. Once the price per unit has been found, a number of items can be deducted in order to determine the customs value. These are, in consecutive order:

1. The commissions usually paid or agreed to be paid or an amount for profit and general expenses which is usual in connection with sales in the country of importation of imported goods of the same class or kind.

The goods of the same class or kind need not come from the same country as the goods being valued.

2. The usual costs of transport and insurance incurred within the country of importation.

3. The costs referred to in article 8, paragraph 2.

As has been mentioned before, article 8, paragraph 2, offers each Party to the Code the opportunity to take, by means of legal provisions, either a c.i.f.- or a f.o.b.-price as the basis for customs valuation. For those countries who have chosen a f.o.b.-price (e.g. the US) the deductive method provides the opportunity to deduct c.i.f.-costs possibly included in the inland resale price, to wit:

a. the cost of transport of the imported goods to the port or place of importation,
b. loading, unloading and handling charges associated with the transport of the imported goods to the port or place of importation, and
c. the cost of insurance.

4. The customs duties and other national taxes payable in the country of importation by reason of the importation or sale of the goods.

D. NO SALE AT OR ABOUT THE TIME OF IMPORTATION

The following solution is provided in case there is no sale at or about the time of importation. During a period of 90 days at the most, starting from the day of importation of the goods being valued, the value may be based on the unit price at which the imported goods or similar imported goods are sold in the country of importation in the condition as imported at the earliest date after the importation of the goods being valued. Once such a unit price has been established, the further procedure is as described under C.

E. SALE AFTER FURTHER PROCESSING OF THE GOODS

Possibly the goods or identical or similar goods are not sold in the condition as imported but only after further processing. In that case the price at which the goods are sold after further processing may be taken as a basis, subject to three conditions:

a. only the price, after processing, of the *imported* goods may be taken into account, and not the price, after processing of identical or similar goods;
b. this line of approach may only be followed at the request of the importer;
c. this method will generally not be applicable if the goods loose their identity as a result of the processing, or if they are such a small part of the processed product that application of this method is not feasible.

There may, however, be cases in which, although the identity is lost, the value added by the processing can be determined accurately and without unreasonable difficulty.

The price, after processing, against which the goods are sold in the greatest aggregate quantity to persons not related to the seller is again decisive.

Apart from the deductible items referred to under C, this method provides for the deduction of the value added by processing. Necessary calculations should be based on objective and quantifiable data.

As regards the loss of identity, since it is impossible to give a general rule it will be necessary to decide on a case by case basis if that has happened.

Chapter 12. The computed value

A. THE METHOD USED

This fifth method of valuation is based on the cost of producing the imported merchandise in the country of production. The usual margin of profit for sales for export to the country of importation should be added to this cost. As the co-operation of the manufacturer in the exporting country will usually be needed to get the necessary data, it seems that this method will only be used if the buyer and seller are related.

The computed value consists of the total of three types of costs.

1. The cost or value of materials and fabrication

This first type relates to the cost or value of materials and manufacture or other processing employed in production.

The cost or value is established on the basis of data which are actually connected to production. The historic costs are decisive; no comparison is made with usual costs. For this reason the manufacturer's accounts should be used, if they satisfy the generally accepted accounting principles in the country where the goods are produced.

The cost or value also includes the cost of packing and packing materials, and the value of goods and services supplied by the buyer free of charge or at a reduced cost. The value of engineering, design work etc. performed in the country of importation will also be included in 'cost or value'. This is different from the first method. However, they will only be included for as much as the producer is actually charged.

2. Profit and general expenses

The second type consists of an amount for profit and general expenses equal to the amount usually reflected in sales of goods for export to the country of importation. This covers the direct and indirect costs of producing and selling the goods as far as they are not already included under the first type.

In this context goods of the same class or kind, produced in the same country as the goods being valued, are concerned. The amount is fixed by means of data supplied by or on behalf of the producer. However, if such data lead to an unusual result, data may be used which are not supplied by the producer.

The amount for profit and general expenses has to be taken as a whole. Only the total has to be in accordance with what is usual. As a result the producer's profit figure may be low while his general expenses may be high (e.g. new products), the total being consistent with what is usually reflected in sales of goods of the same class or kind.

This again illustrates the 'positive' approach in the Code, as opposed to a 'notional' concept. In the note it is stated that 'where the producer can demonstrate that he is taking a low profit on his sales of the imported goods because of particular commercial circumstances, his actual profit figures should be taken into account provided that he has valid commercial reasons to justify them and his pricing policy reflects usual pricing policies in the branch of industry concerned'. We feel a similar approach may be defended if there is no profit or even a loss.

3. Cost associated with the transport

The cost of transport and associated costs up to the point of entry will be included in- or excluded from the computed value, depending on the choice made by the Party to the Code between c.i.f. and f.o.b.

B. INFORMATION

If the customs administration makes use of data other than those supplied by the producer in order to establish the computed value, the producer must at his request be informed of the provenance and the calculations made on the basis of those data. Article 10 of the Code, which guarantees the confidentiality of certain data supplied to the customs administration, should, however, be kept in mind. It is stated in the second paragraph of article 6 that the customs administration cannot force anyone not resident in the territory of importation to supply data or to allow an inquiry in order to determinate the computed value.

The customs administration can only verify certain data in another country with the permission of the person who supplied those data. The permission of the government of the country concerned is also required beforehand.

It is doubtful when one looks at these provisions that the use of this method of valuation will assume large proportions. Nevertheless it may work to the advantage of producers if they are willing to co-operate with the customs administration.

Chapter 13. The flexible valuation method

If none of the previous methods has proved applicable, the customs value should be established by means of the flexible valuation method.

To this end the customs administration can make use of 'reasonable means consistent with the principles and general provisions of the Code and of article VII of the GATT'.

Only data which are available in the country of importation may, however, be used.

The note to this article clarifies what is meant by this vague wording. It contains two important conditions:

a. Customs values determined under the provisions of this method should, to the greatest extent possible, be based on previously determined customs values;

b. Making use of 'reasonable means' is to say that the previous five methods should again be tried consecutively, but this time with a reasonable flexibility.

The following examples of such a flexibility may be given:

1. *identical goods*: identical imported goods produced in a country other than the country of exportation of the goods being valued could be the basis for customs valuation;
2. *similar goods*: the requirement that the similar goods should be exported at or about the same time as the goods being valued could be flexibly interpreted;
3. *the deductive method*: the 'ninety days' requirement could be administered flexibly.

Furthermore, application of the flexible valuation method may not result in any of the situations enumerated in article 7.

These include:

a. the fixing of the value on the basis of arbitrary or fictitious values;

b. the value being fixed by making use of the price of the goods for export to a country other than the country of importation;

c. the value being fixed by means of the selling price on the home-market of goods produced in the importing country (e.g. the old American Selling Price System).

Chapter 14. Other methods for customs valuation

In the following we wish to give an impression of the great diversity of systems for customs valuation. We wil not, however, enter into details, as the purpose of this book is discussing the GATT-Code, which is already (or will probably be in the near future) in use in the most important trading countries. Apart from this we will pay some attention to the so-called 'Brussels definition of value' because it will 'govern the market' together with the Code during the coming years. The most important differences between these systems will be pointed out.

An agreement on the principles of customs valuation was reached in a broad international context for the first time in 1947.

This led to the conclusion of article VII of the GATT, which has been discussed in chapter 5. The principles are applied by roughly 80 GATT-members, while there are in fact a dozen other countries which apply the GATT-rules.

As has been mentioned before, the GATT-principles do not contain a complete system of valuation of goods for customs purposes, while the countries are left too much freedom in the practical application.

This led to the conclusion of the Brussels Convention on the valuation of goods in 1950, in which the GATT-rules were developed into the so-called Brussels definition of value. This convention was placed under the administration of the Customs Co-operation Council.

The countries applying the Brussels definition of value in 1979 took care of roughly 60% of world-imports.

Out of these countries roughly 30 had joined the Brussels Convention of value, while about 65 of them had based their valuation-systems on this convention to a greater or lesser extent, without joining. Particularly the US, Canada and most Asiatic countries used other systems of valuation.

The system of valuation of goods for customs purposes which was applied in the US up to the first of July 1980 in fact consisted of six different subsystems. Which system was actually used depended on the imported merchandise. Each system contained 'standards'. Of a total of nine standards seven were based on the price of the goods in the country of exportation and two were based on the American Selling Price (ASP) of the domestic counterpart of the imported article. Where the standard was based on the price in the exporting country either the value of goods sold for export to the US or the value of goods sold for domestic consumption was used. This system, which was replaced by the GATT-Code on the first of July 1980, was not easy to understand and received a lot of criticism from abroad.

Australia also used a system which was not very transparent. This system was replaced fairly recently by the Brussels definition of value. In brief, the Australian system took either the transaction value on a f.o.b.-basis or the price for which the goods were sold for domestic consumption in the exporting country, whichever was the higher, as the customs value. These prices were adjusted to some extent. As far as known, such a system is still in use in Zimbabwe.

In Brazil a system based on the invoice prices is commonly used, but for a large number of goods (about 10% of imports) minimum values or basic prices are used. In favour of this Brazil argues that this is generally done to combat fraud, while the system is also applied to goods with prices which are difficult to fix or which fluctuate.

Canada takes the home-market price in the exporting country as a basis for customs valuation.

Marocco uses the Maroccan wholesale price, minus taxes.

Mexico makes use of a system in which either the invoice amount (on a f.o.b.-basis) or an official price established by the Mexican authorities is used, whichever is the higher. The official prices are almost always higher than the transacted price. The protection of the home-market is clearly the purpose of this system.

Paraguay takes the f.o.b.-value as a point of departure, and adds 20%, while Uruguay applies c.i.f.-values which have been officially fixed by the administration.

The Soviet Union uses the exporting country's wholesale prices to which all costs up to the point of entry are added for other than state purchases. For private imports the retail price in the Soviet Union is used.

Hardly any data are available on several countries, especially Asiatic ones.

However, the Brussels definition of value is still used at least as the basis for systems of valuation in a large number of countries. A closer look at this system seems justified.

Chapter 15. The Brussels definition of value

A. DEFINITION

As has been noted before (in chapter 2, point B), a definition of value will either be based on a positive concept (as is the Code) or a notional concept. While the Brussels definition of value is based on a notional concept, the attempt has been made to approach normal trade practice whenever possible. At the time the system was conceived it was argued in favour of a notional concept that the customs administration would be more able to combat fraud, while the importer acting in good faith would be free from protectionist measures. When the definition was drawn up it was believed it met the needs of the trade, which had called for a simple and comprehensive system.

In this definition (included as annex 2):

1. the price is taken which results from a (if necessary: theoretical) sale and purchase:

a. which concerns the goods imported and

b. is made under open market conditions between a buyer and a seller who are independent of each other;

2. the standard is further specified by stating the sale and purchase should have resulted in a price which:

c. is valid at the time the duty becomes payable and for which

d. the merchandise is delivered to the buyer at the place of introduction (in the country of importation).

It can be seen that the definition is based on a notional concept. A price can only be accepted if the above conditions *a* to *d* have been met.

The definition consists of no more than a total of three articles. Article I contains the basis. There it is stated that 'for the purpose of levying ad valorem duties of customs the value of any goods imported for home use shall be taken to be the price which they would fetch at the time when the duty becomes payable on a sale in the open market between a buyer and a seller independent of each other'.

In order to find this price, it is assumed the goods are delivered to the buyer at the point where the merchandise enters the importing country. Furthermore, the assumption is made that the buyer bears all the costs related to the sale and delivery at the place of introduction (e.g. costs of transport, insurance, commission, brokerage). Duties and taxes levied in the country of importation are not included in the price.

Article II provides a definition of a sale/purchase under conditions of free competition. Such is the case if the price has not been influenced by any commercial, financial or other special relationship between the seller and buyer and if there is no special connection between them.

Article III concerns patents, trade-marks, designs etc. The value of the right to use them should be included in the price.

B. ELEMENTS

Using a different approach, the following elements may be recognised in the Brussels definition of value.

1. Time

The value of the goods should be established according to the existing situation at the moment they are imported. However, as some time usually passes between the conclusion of the contract and the introduction into the importing country a degree of tolerance is accorded in respect of this time element.

2. Place

Goods are valued on the assumption that all costs incidental to the sale and delivery to the place of introduction into the country of importation are included. This corresponds to the c.i.f.-value.

3. Quantity and level of transaction

The value of the imported merchandise is the value corresponding to the number of goods being valued, sold at the same level (wholesale, manufacturer etc.). This is important because of quantity or wholesale discounts.

4. Open market conditions

Under these conditions the payment of the price agreed is the sole consideration. The price should in no way have been influenced by a commercial, financial or any other special relationship between buyer and seller and no share of the proceeds of a subsequent resale by the buyer should accrue to the seller in any way.

In cases where the transaction value lies (well) below the price for which identical or similar goods are bought by other buyers this leads to the result that the price is 'uplifted' to obtain the normal price. The market price of the imported goods in the importing country used to be the starting point for this procedure.

5. Patents and foreign trade-marks

The value of merchandise manufactured in accordance with a patented invention (drawings, models etc.) or imported under a foreign trade-mark, is fixed by including the value of this patent or trade-mark.

In order to avoid in daily practice having to compare every price to the theoretical standard described above, it has been made possible to accept the price which has actually been agreed as the basis for fixing the customs value as long as it is genuine and if some corrections are made.

C. PRACTICAL APPLICATION

Taking all of this into account, the Brussels definition of value does not seem unattractive. However, during the period of its application disputes concerning the level of the transaction, advertising costs, various discounts etc. arose in many countries. In particular, the Brussels definition of value was found to leave open several possibilities for practising protectionism if the countries wished to do so. It was apparent too often, that up-lifts, price-lists etc. were being used in order to fix a value which was totally different from the actual price. This was made possible by applying the criterion: 'the price the goods would fetch . . .'

Chapter 16. Differences in valuation between the Code and the Brussels definition of value

A. PRICE

The Code and the Brussels definition of value are the systems which are applied the most (taking the volume of trade concerned into account). Because of this it is important to point out the essential differences between these two systems.

As has been mentioned before, the GATT-Code is based on a positive concept, while the Brussels definition is founded on a notional concept. While the possibility to accept the price which has actually been agreed (if genuine and if the prescribed adjustments have been made) as the basis for the valuation has been included in the Brussels definition, this price is often tested by comparing it to usual open market price. In other words, the customs administration will check if the price is 'normal'.

If the Code is applied this does not happen, as the transaction value is taken as the starting-point without any restrictions (as long as it has not been influenced by any special relationship between buyer and seller).

B. QUANTITY

Another difference lies in the way in which 'quantity' is treated. While this element has been developed into a complete doctrine in the countries using the Brussels definition, it does not play any role in the Code at all.

In particular, this leads to different results if, say, ten thousand units of a product are purchased on the world-market and a thousand of them are imported into one particular country. If the Code is applicable the value is taken to be one tenth of the total value. However, those who use the Brussels definition will have to ask themselves what price would have been paid if only a thousand units had been bought. Obviously, this price would have been higher than one tenth of the price of ten thousand units.

C. LEVEL OF THE TRANSACTION

In the level of the transaction – the place in the supplychain filled by the importer – another important difference is found. This is one of the elements determining the normal price in the Brussels definition of value. In case of a sale to a buyer related to the seller one will have to ask oneself if any transactions are normally made between unrelated parties at such a level. This at least used to be the Dutch doctrine. This element is of no consequence in the Code.

D. SECONDARY UNDERTAKINGS

The Brussels definition makes the assumption, that secondary undertakings such as providing warranty, advertising etc. have influenced the price. As a result, the value of such undertakings has to be included in the price. In countries applying the Code, however, the value of such undertakings is not included in the customs value.

E. THE PLACE WHERE THE BUYER IS ESTABLISHED

One of the most important differences between the Brussels definition of value and the GATT-Code concerns the place where the buyer has his establishment. Many countries using the Brussels definition make the condition that the buyer should be established in the country of importation. The Code, however, clearly shows the American influence. As it is not unusual that Americans run their businesses in the US from for instance the Bahama's, it has not been stipulated that the buyer should be established in the country of importation.

F. DISCOUNTS AND OTHER PRICE-REDUCTIONS

Under the provisions of the Brussels definition discounts and other price-reductions are tested by a comparison with whatever is customary in the line of business concerned, e.g. reduction on account of the level at which the transaction is made, or the quantity purchased. This poses no problems to countries applying the Code. They will accept any discount or other reduction in price as long as these have not been influenced by a relation between the buyer and the seller.

Annex 1. Art. VII of the GATT

(GENERAL AGREEMENT ON TARIFFS AND TRADE)

ARTICLE VII

Valuation for Customs Purposes

1. The contracting parties recognize the validity of the general principles of valuation set forth in the following paragraphs of this Article, and they undertake to give effect to such principles, in respect of all products subject to duties or other charges or restrictions on importation and exportation based upon or regulated in any manner by value. Moreover, they shall, upon a request by another contracting party review the operation of any of their laws or regulations relating to value for customs purposes in the light of these principles. THE CONTRACTING PARTIES[1] may request from contracting parties reports on steps taken by them in pursuance of the provisions of this Article.

2. *a*. The value for customs purposes of imported merchandise should be based on the actual value of the imported merchandise on which duty is assessed, or of like merchandise, and should not be based on the value of merchandise of national origin or on arbitrary or fictitious values.

b. 'Actual value' should be the price at which, at a time and place determined by the legislation of the country of importation, such or like merchandise is sold or offered for sale in the ordinary course of trade under fully competitive conditions. To the extent to which the price of such or like merchandise is governed by the quantity in a particular transaction, the price to be considered should uniformly be related to either (i) comparable quantities, or (ii) quantities not less favourable to importers than those in which the greater volume of the

1. CONTRACTING PARTIES, i.e. the contracting parties acting jointly as provided for in Article XXV of the GATT.

merchandise is sold in the trade between the countries of exportation and importation.

c. When the actual value is not ascertainable in accordance with sub-paragraph b of this paragraph, the value for customs purposes should be based on the nearest ascertainable equivalent of such value.

3. The value for customs purposes of any imported product should not include the amount of any internal tax, applicable within the country of origin or export, from which the imported product has been exempted or has been or will be relieved by means of refund.

4. *a*. Except as otherwise provided for in this paragraph, where it is necessary for the purposes of paragraph 2 of this Article for a contracting party to convert into its own currency a price expressed in the currency of another country, the conversion rate of exchange to be used shall be based, for each currency involved, on the par value as established pursuant to the Articles of Agreement of the International Monetary Fund or on the rate of exchange recognized by the Fund, or on the par value established in accordance with a special exchange agreement entered into pursuant to Article XV of this Agreement.

b. Where no such established par value and no such recognized rate of exchange exist, the conversion rate shall reflect effectively the current value of such currency in commercial transactions.

c. The CONTRACTING PARTIES, in agreement with the International Monetary Fund, shall formulate rules governing the conversion by contracting parties of any foreign currency in respect of which multiple rates of exchange are maintained consistently with the Articles of Agreement of the International Monetary Fund. Any contracting party may apply such rules in respect of such foreign currencies for the purposes of paragraph 2 of this Article as an alternative to the use of par values. Until such rules are adopted by the CONTRACTING PARTIES, any contracting party may employ, in respect of any such foreign currency, rules of conversion for the purposes of paragraph 2 of this Article which are designed to reflect effectively the value of such foreign currency in commercial transactions.

d. Nothing in this paragraph shall be construed to require any contracting party to alter the method of converting currencies for customs purposes which is applicable in its territory on the date of this Agreement, if such alteration would have the effect of increasing generally the amounts of duty payable.

5. The bases and methods for determining the value of products subject to duties or other charges or restrictions based upon or regulated in any manner by value should be stable and should be given sufficient publicity to enable

traders to estimate, with a reasonable degree of certainty, the value for customs purposes.

NOTE TO ARTICLE VII

Paragraph I

The expression 'or other charges' is not to be regarded as including internal taxes or equivalent charges imposed on or in connexion with imported products.

Paragraph 2

1. It would be in conformity with Article VII to presume that 'actual value' may be represented by the invoice price, plus any non-included charges for legitimate costs which are proper elements of 'actual value' and plus any abnormal discount or other reduction from the ordinary competitive price.

2. It would be in conformity with Article VII, paragraph 2.*b* for a contracting party to construe the phrase 'in the ordinary course of trade . . . under fully competitive conditions', as excluding any transaction wherein the buyer and seller are not independent of each other and price is not the sole consideration.

3. The standard of 'fully competitive conditions' permits a contracting party to exclude from consideration prices involving special discounts limited to exclusive agents.

4. The wording of sub-paragraphs *a* and *b* permits a contracting party to determine the value for customs purposes uniformly either (1) on the basis of a particular exporter's prices of the imported merchandise, or (2) on the basis of the general price level of like merchandise.

Annex 2. The Brussels definition of value

(ANNEX I TO THE CONVENTION ON THE VALUATION OF GOODS FOR CUSTOMS PURPOSES)

DEFINITION OF VALUE

ARTICLE I

1. For the purposes of levying ad valorem duties of customs, the value of any goods imported for home use shall be taken to be the normal price, that is to say, the price which they would fetch at the time when the duty becomes payable on a sale in the open market between a buyer and a seller independent of each other.

2. The normal price of any imported goods shall be determined on the following assumptions:

a. that the goods are delivered to the buyer at the port or place of introduction into the country of importation;

b. that the seller bears all costs, charges and expenses incidental to the sale and to the delivery of the goods at the port or place of introduction, which are hence included in the normal price;

c. that the buyer bears any duties or taxes applicable in the country of importation, which are hence not included in the normal price.

ARTICLE II

1. A sale in the open market between a buyer and a seller independent of each other pre-supposes:

a. that the price is the sole consideration;

b. that the price is not influenced by any commercial, financial or other relationship, whether by contract or otherwise, between the seller or any person associated in business with him and the buyer or any person associated in business with him, other than the relationship created by the sale itself;

c. that no part of the proceeds of any subsequent resale, other disposal or use of the goods will accrue, either directly or indirectly, to the seller or any person associated in business with him.

2. Two persons shall be deemed to be associated in business with one another if, whether directly or indirectly, either of them has any interest in the business or property of the other or both have a common interest in any business or property or some third person has an interest in the business or property of both of them.

ARTICLE III

When the goods to be valued:

a. are manufactured in accordance with any patented invention or are goods to which any protected design has been applied; or

b. are imported under a foreign trade mark; or

c. are imported for sale, other disposal or use under a foreign trade mark,

the normal price shall be determined on the assumption that it includes the value of the right to use the patent, design or trade mark in respect of the goods.

Annex 3. The Code

(AGREEMENT ON IMPLEMENTATION OF ARTICLE VII OF THE GENERAL AGREEMENT ON TARIFFS AND TRADE)

GENERAL INTRODUCTORY COMMENTARY

1. The primary basis for customs value under this Agreement is 'transaction value' as defined in Article 1. Article 1 is to be read together with Article 8 which provides, *inter alia*, for adjustments to the price actually paid or payable in cases where certain specific elements which are considered to form a part of the value for customs purposes are incurred by the buyer but are not included in the price actually paid or payable for the imported goods. Article 8 also provides for the inclusion in the transaction value of certain considerations which may pass from the buyer to the seller in the form of specified goods or services rather than in the form of money. Articles 2 to 7, inclusive, provide methods of determining the customs value whenever it cannot be determined under the provisions of Article 1.

2. Where the customs value cannot be determined under the provisions of Article 1 there should normally be a process of consultation between the customs administration and importer with a view to arriving at a basis of value under the provisions of Articles 2 or 3. It may occur, for example, that the importer has information about the customs value of identical or similar imported goods which is not immediately available to the customs administration in the port of importation. On the other hand, the customs administration may have information about the customs value of identical or similar imported goods which is not readily available to the importer. A process of consultation between the two parties will enable information to be exchanged, subject to the requirements of commercial confidentiality, with a view to determining a proper basis of value for customs purposes.

3. Articles 5 and 6 provide two bases for determining the customs value where

it cannot be determined on the basis of the transaction value of the imported goods or of identical or similar imported goods. Under Article 5.1 the customs value is determined on the basis of the price at which the goods are sold in the condition as imported to an unrelated buyer in the country of importation. The importer also has the right to have goods which are further processed after importation valued under the provisions of Article 5 if he so requests. Under Article 6 the customs value is determined on the basis of the computed value. Both these methods present certain difficulties and because of this the importer is given the right, under the provisions of Article 4, to choose the order of application of the two methods.

4. Article 7 sets out how to determine the customs value in cases where it cannot be determined under the provisions of any of the preceding Articles.

PREAMBLE

Having regard to the Multilateral Trade Negotiations, the Parties to this Agreement (hereinafter referred to as 'Parties'),

Desiring to further the objectives of the General Agreement on Tariffs and Trade (hereinafter referred to as 'General Agreement' or 'GATT') and to secure additional benefits for the international trade of developing countries;

Recognizing the importance of the provisions of Article VII of the General Agreement and desiring to elaborate rules for their application in order to provide greater uniformity and certainty in their implementation;

Recognizing the need for a fair, uniform and neutral system for the valuation of goods for customs purposes that precludes the use of arbitrary or fictitious customs values;

Recognizing that the basis for valuation of goods for customs purposes should, to the greatest extent possible, be the transaction value of the goods being valued;

Recognizing that customs value should be based on simple and equitable criteria consistent with commercial practices and that valuation procedures should be of general application without distinction between sources of supply;

Recognizing that valuation procedures should not be used to combat dumping;

Hereby agree as follows:

PART I

RULES ON CUSTOMS VALUATION

Article 1

1. The customs value of imported goods shall be the transaction value, that is the price actually paid or payable for the goods when sold for export to the country of importation adjusted in accordance with the provisions of Article 8, provided:

a. that there are no restrictions as to the disposition or use of the goods by the buyer other than restrictions which:
   (i) are imposed or required by law or by the public authorities in the country of importation;
   (ii) limit the geographical area in which the goods may be resold; or
   (iii) do not substantially affect the value of the goods;

b. that the sale or price is not subject to some condition or consideration for which a value cannot be determined with respect to the goods being valued;

c. that no part of the proceeds of any subsequent resale, disposal or use of the goods by the buyer will accrue directly or indirectly to the seller, unless an appropriate adjustment can be made in accordance with the provisions of Article 8; and

d. that the buyer and seller are not related, or where the buyer and seller are related, that the transaction value is acceptable for customs purposes under the provisions of paragraph 2 of this Article.

2.*a.* In determining whether the transaction value is acceptable for the purposes of paragraph 1, the fact that the buyer and the seller are related within the meaning of Article 15 shall not in itself be grounds for regarding the transaction value as unacceptable. In such case the circumstances surrounding the sale shall be examined and the transaction value shall be accepted provided that the relationship did not influence the price. If, in the light of information provided by the importer or otherwise, the customs administration has grounds for considering that the relationship influenced the price, it shall communicate its grounds to the importer and he shall be given a reasonable opportunity to respond. If the importer so requests, the communication of the grounds shall be in writing.

b. In a sale between related persons, the transaction value shall be accepted and the goods valued in accordance with the provisions of paragraph 1 whenever the importer demonstrates that such value closely approximates to one of the following occurring at or about the same time:

(i) the transaction value in sales to unrelated buyers of identical or similar goods for export to the same country of importation;

(ii) the customs value of identical or similar goods as determined under the provisions of Article 5;

(iii) the customs value of identical or similar goods as determined under the provisions of Article 6;

(iv) the transaction value in sales to unrelated buyers for export to the same country of importation of goods which would be identical to the imported goods except for having a different country of production provided that the sellers in any two transactions being compared are not related.[1]

In applying the foregoing tests, due account shall be taken of demonstrated differences in commercial levels, quantity levels, the elements enumerated in Article 8 and costs incurred by the seller in sales in which he and the buyer are not related that are not incurred by the seller in sales in which he and the buyer are related.

c. The tests set forth in paragraph 2.*b* are to be used at the initiative of the importer and only for comparison purposes. Substitute values may not be established under the provisions of paragraph 2.

Article 2

1.*a.* If the customs value of the imported goods cannot be determined under the provisions of Article 1, the customs value shall be the transaction value of identical goods sold for export to the same country of importation and exported at or about the same time as the goods being valued.

b. In applying this Article, the transaction value of identical goods in a sale at the same commercial level and in substantially the same quantity as the goods being valued shall be used to determine the customs value. Where no such sale is found, the transaction value of identical goods sold at a different commercial level and/or in different quantities, adjusted to take account of differences attributable to commercial level and/or to quantity, shall be used, provided that such adjustments can be made on the basis of demonstrated evidence which clearly establishes the reasonableness and accuracy of the adjustment, whether the adjustment leads to an increase or a decrease in the value.

1. This fourth test-value has been deleted by acceptance of the protocol to the Code.

2. Where the costs and charges referred to in Article 8.2 are included in the transaction value, an adjustment shall be made to take account of significant differences in such costs and charges between the imported goods and the identical goods in question arising from differences in distances and modes of transport.

3. If, in applying this Article, more than one transaction value of identical goods is found, the lowest such value shall be used to determine the customs value of the imported goods.

Article 3

1.*a.* If the customs value of the imported goods cannot be determined under the provisions of Articles 1 and 2, the customs value shall be the transaction value of similar goods sold for export to the same country of importation and exported at or about the same time as the goods being valued.

b. In applying this Article, the transaction value of similar goods in a sale at the same commercial level and in substantially the same quantity as the goods being valued shall be used to determine the customs value. Where no such sale is found, the transaction value of similar goods sold at a different commercial level and/or in different quantities, adjusted to take account of differences attributable to commercial level and/or to quantity, shall be used, provided that such adjustments can be made on the basis of demonstrated evidence which clearly establishes the reasonableness and accuracy of the adjustment, whether the adjustment leads to an increase or a decrease in the value.

2. Where the costs and charges referred to in Article 8.2 are included in the transaction value, an adjustment shall be made to take account of significant differences in such costs and charges between the imported goods and the similar goods in question arising from differences in distances and modes of transport.

3. If, in applying this Article, more than one transaction value of similar goods is found, the lowest such value shall be used to determine the customs value of the imported goods.

Article 4

If the customs value of the imported goods cannot be determined under the provisions of Articles 1, 2 and 3 the customs value shall be determined under the provisions of Article 5 or, when the customs value cannot be determined under that Article, under the provisions of Article 6 except that, at the request of the importer, the order of application of Articles 5 and 6 shall be reversed.

Article 5

1.*a*. If the imported goods or identical or similar imported goods are sold in the country of importation in the condition as imported, the customs value of the imported goods under the provisions of this Article shall be based on the unit price at which the imported goods or identical or similar imported goods are so sold in the greatest aggregate quantity, at or about the time of the importation of the goods being valued, to persons who are not related to the persons from whom they buy such goods, subject to deductions for the following:

(i) either the commissions usually paid or agreed to be paid or the additions usually made for profit and general expenses in connexion with sales in such country of imported goods of the same class or kind;

(ii) the usual costs of transport and insurance and associated costs incurred within the country of importation;

(iii) where appropriate, the costs and charges referred to in Article 8.2; and

(iv) the customs duties and other national taxes payable in the country of importation by reason of the importation or sale of the goods.

b. If neither the imported goods nor identical nor similar imported goods are sold at or about the time of importation of the goods being valued, the customs value shall, subject otherwise to the provisions of paragraph 1.*a* of this Article, be based on the unit price at which the imported goods or identical or similar imported goods are sold in the country of importation in the condition as imported at the earliest date after the importation of the goods being valued but before the expiration of ninety days after such importation.

2. If neither the imported goods nor identical nor similar imported goods are sold in the country of importation in the condition as imported, then, if the importer so requests, the customs value shall be based on the unit price at which the imported goods, after further processing, are sold in the greatest aggregate quantity to persons in the country of importation who are not related to the persons from whom they buy such goods, due allowance being made for the value added by such processing and the deductions provided for in paragraph 1.*a* of this Article.

Article 6

1. The customs value of imported goods under the provisions of this Article shall be based on a computed value. Computed value shall consist of the sum of:

a. the cost or value of materials and fabrication or other processing employed in producing the imported goods;

b. an amount for profit and general expenses equal to that usually reflected in sales of goods of the same class or kind as the goods being valued which are made by producers in the country of exportation for export to the country of importation;

c. the cost or value of all other expenses necessary to reflect the valuation option chosen by the Party under Article 8.2.

2. No Party may require or compel any person not resident in its own territory to produce for examination, or to allow access to, any account or other record for the purposes of determining a computed value. However, information supplied by the producer of the goods for the purposes of determining the customs value under the provisions of this Article may be verified in another country by the authorities of the country of importation with the agreement of the producer and provided they give sufficient advance notice to the government of the country in question and the latter does not object to the investigation.

Article 7

1. If the customs value of the imported goods cannot be determined under the provisions of Articles 1 to 6, inclusive, the customs value shall be determined using reasonable means consistent with the principles and general provisions of this Agreement and of Article VII of the General Agreement and on the basis of data available in the country of importation.

2. No customs value shall be determined under the provisions of this Article on the basis of:

a. the selling price in the country of importation of goods produced in such country;

b. a system which provides for the acceptance for customs purposes of the higher of two alternative values;

c. the price of goods on the domestic market of the country of exportation;

d. the cost of production other than computed values which have been determined for identical or similar goods in accordance with the provisions of Article 6;

e. the price of the goods for export to a country other than the country of importation;

f. minimum customs values; or

g. arbitrary or fictitious values.

3. If he so requests, the importer shall be informed in writing of the customs value determined under the provisions of this Article and the method used to determine such value.

Article 8

1. In determining the customs value under the provisions of Article 1, there shall be added to the price actually paid or payable for the imported goods:

a. the following, to the extent that they are incurred by the buyer but are not included in the price actually paid or payable for the goods:
   (i) commissions and brokerage, except buying commissions;
   (ii) the cost of containers which are treated as being one for customs purposes with the goods in question;
   (iii) the cost of packing whether for labour or materials;

b. the value, apportioned as appropriate, of the following goods and services where supplied directly or indirectly by the buyer free of charge or at reduced cost for use in connexion with the production and sale for export of the imported goods, to the extent that such value has not been included in the price actually paid or payable:
   (i) materials, components, parts and similar items incorporated in the imported goods;
   (ii) tools, dies, moulds and similar items used in the production of the imported goods;
   (iii) materials consumed in the production of the imported goods;
   (iv) engineering, development, artwork, design work, and plans and sketches undertaken elsewhere than in the country of importation and necessary for the production of the imported goods;

c. royalties and licence fees related to the goods being valued that the buyer must pay, either directly or indirectly, as a condition of sale of the goods being valued, to the extent that such royalties and fees are not included in the price actually paid or payable;

d. the value of any part of the proceeds of any subsequent resale, disposal or use of the imported goods that accrues directly or indirectly to the seller.

2. In framing its legislation, each Party shall provide for the inclusion in or the exclusion from the customs value, in whole or in part, of the following:
a. the cost of transport of the imported goods to the port or place of importation;
b. loading, unloading and handling charges associated with the transport of the imported goods to the port or place of importation; and
c. the cost of insurance.

3. Additions to the price actually paid or payable shall be made under this Article only on the basis of objective and quantifiable data.

4. No additions shall be made to the price actually paid or payable in determining the customs value except as provided in this Article.

Article 9

1. Where the conversion of currency is necessary for the determination of the customs value, the rate of exchange to be used shall be that duly published by the competent authorities of the country of importation concerned and shall reflect as effectively as possible, in respect of the period covered by each such document of publication, the current value of such currency in commercial transactions in terms of the currency of the country of importation.

2. The conversion rate to be used shall be that in effect at the time of exportation or the time of importation, as provided by each Party.

Article 10

All information which is by nature confidential or which is provided on a confidential basis for the purposes of customs valuation shall be treated as strictly confidential by the authorities concerned who shall not disclose it without the specific permission of the person or government providing such information, except to the extent that it may be required to be disclosed in the context of judicial proceedings.

Article 11

1. The legislation of each Party shall provide in regard to a determination of

customs value for the right to appeal, without penalty, by the importer or any other person liable for the payment of the duty.

2. An initial right of appeal without penalty may be to an authority within the customs administration or to an independent body, but the legislation of each Party shall provide for the right of appeal without penalty to a judicial authority.

3. Notice of the decision on appeal shall be given to the appellant and the reasons for such decision shall be provided in writing. He shall also be informed of his rights of any further appeal.

Article 12

Laws, regulations, judicial decisions and administrative rulings of general application giving effect to this Agreement shall be published in conformity with Article X of the General Agreement by the country of importation concerned.

Article 13

If, in the course of determining the customs value of imported goods, it becomes necessary to delay the final determination of such customs value, the importer shall nevertheless be able to withdraw his goods from customs if, where so required, he provides sufficient guarantee in the form of a surety, a deposit or some other appropriate instrument, covering the ultimate payment of customs duties for which the goods may be liable. The legislation of each Party shall make provisions for such circumstances.

Article 14

The notes at Annex I to this Agreement form an integral part of this Agreement and the Articles of this Agreement are to be read and applied in conjunction with their respective notes. Annexes II and III also form an integral part of this Agreement.[1]

1. Annexes I, II and III are not included in this annex.

Article 15

1. In this Agreement:
a. 'customs value of imported goods' means the value of goods for the purposes of levying ad valorem duties of customs on imported goods;
b. 'country of importation' means country or customs territory of importation; and
c. 'produced' includes grown, manufactured and mined.

2. *a*. In this Agreement 'identical goods' means goods which are the same in all respects, including physical characteristics, quality and reputation. Minor differences in appearance would not preclude goods otherwise conforming to the definition from being regarded as identical.
b. In this Agreement 'similar goods' means goods which, although not alike in all respects, have like characteristics and like component materials which enable them to perform the same functions and to be commercially interchangeable. The quality of the goods, their reputation and the existence of a trademark are among the factors to be considered in determining whether goods are similar.
c. The terms 'identical goods' and 'similar goods' do not include, as the case may be, goods which incorporate or reflect engineering, development, artwork, design work, and plans and sketches for which no adjustment has been made under Article 8.1 (*b*)(iv) because such elements were undertaken in the country of importation.
d. Goods shall not be regarded as 'identical goods' or 'similar goods' unless they were produced in the same country as the goods being valued.
e. Goods produced by a different person shall be taken into account only when there are no identical goods or similar goods, as the case may be, produced by the same person as the goods being valued.

3. In this Agreement 'goods of the same class or kind' means goods which fall within a group or range of goods produced by a particular industry or industry sector, and includes identical or similar goods.

4. For the purposes of this Agreement, persons shall be deemed to be related only if:
a. they are officers or directors of one another's businesses;
b. they are legally recognized partners in business;
c. they are employer and employee;
d. any person directly or indirectly owns, controls or holds 5 percent or more of the outstanding voting stock or shares of both of them;

e. one of them directly or indirectly controls the other;
f. both of them are directly or indirectly controlled by a third person;
g. together they directly or indirectly control a third person; or
h. they are members of the same family.

5. Persons who are associated in business with one another in that one is the sole agent, sole distributor or sole concessionaire, however described, of the other shall be deemed to be related for the purposes of this Agreement if they fall within the criteria of paragraph 4 of this Article.

Article 16

Upon written request, the importer shall have the right to an explanation in writing from the customs administration of the country of importation as to how the customs value of his imported goods was determined.

Article 17

Nothing in this Agreement shall be construed as restricting or calling into question the rights of customs administrations to satisfy themselves as to the truth or accuracy of any statement, document or declaration presented for customs valuation purposes.

PART II

ADMINISTRATION, CONSULTATION AND DISPUTE SETTLEMENT

Institutions

Article 18

There shall be established under this Agreement:

1. A Committee on Customs Valuation (hereinafter referred to as the Committee) composed of representatives from each of the Parties. The Committee shall elect its own Chairman and shall normally meet once a year, or as is otherwise envisaged by the relevant provisions of this Agreement, for the purpose of affording Parties the opportunity to consult on matters relating to the ad-

ministration of the customs valuation system by any Party as it might affect the operation of this Agreement or the furtherance of its objectives and carrying out such other responsibilities as may be assigned to it by the Parties. The GATT secretariat shall act as the secretariat to the Committee.

2. A Technical Committee on Customs Valuation (hereinafter referred to as the Technical Committee) under the auspices of the Customs Cooperation Council, which shall carry out the responsibilities described in Annex II to this Agreement and shall operate in accordance with the rules of procedure contained therein.

Consultation

Article 19

1. If any Party considers that any benefit accruing to it, directly or indirectly, under this Agreement is being nullified or impaired, or that the achievement of any objective of this Agreement is being impeded, as a result of the actions of another Party or of other Parties, it may, with a view to reaching a mutually satisfactory solution of the matter, request consultations with the Party or Parties in question. Each Party shall afford sympathetic consideration to any request from another Party for consultations.

2. The Parties concerned shall initiate requested consultations promptly.

3. Parties engaged in consultations on a particular matter affecting the operation of this Agreement shall attempt to conclude such consultations within a reasonably short period of time. The Technical Committee shall provide, upon request, advice and assistance to Parties engaged in consultations.

Dispute settlement

Article 20

1. If no mutually satisfactory solution has been reached between the Parties concerned in consultations under Article 19 above, the Committee shall meet at the request of any party to the dispute, within thirty days of receipt of such a request, to investigate the matter, with a view to facilitating a mutually satisfactory solution.

2. In investigating the matter and in selecting its procedures, the Committee shall take into account whether the issues in dispute relate to commercial policy considerations or to questions requiring detailed technical consideration. The Committee may request on its own initiative that the Technical Committee carry out an examination, as provided in paragraph 4 below, of any question requiring technical consideration. Upon the request of any party to the dispute that considers the issues to relate to questions of a technical nature, the Committee shall request the Technical Committee to carry out such an examination.

3. During any phase of a dispute settlement procedure, competent bodies and experts in matters under consideration may be consulted; appropriate information and assistance may be requested from such bodies and experts. The Committee shall take into consideration the results of any work of the Technical Committee that pertain to the matter in dispute.

Technical issues

4. When the Technical Committee is requested under the provisions of paragraph 2 above, it shall examine the matter and report to the Committee no later than three months from the date the technical issue was referred to it, unless the period is extended by mutual agreement between the parties to the dispute.

Panel proceedings

5. In cases where the matter is not referred to the Technical Committee, the Committee shall establish a panel upon the request of any party to the dispute if no mutually satisfactory solution has been reached within three months from the date of the request to the Committee to investigate the matter. Where the matter is referred to the Technical Committee, the Committee shall establish a panel upon the request of any party to the dispute if no mutually satisfactory solution has been reached within one month from the date when the Technical Committee presents its report to the Committee.

6. *a*. When a panel is established, it shall be governed by the procedures as set forth in Annex III.

b. If the Technical Committee has made a report on the technical aspects of the matter in dispute, the panel shall use this report as the basis for its consideration of the technical aspects of the matter in dispute.

Enforcement

7. After the investigation is completed or after the report of the Technical Committee or panel is presented to the Committee, the Committee shall give the matter prompt consideration. With respect to panel reports, the Committee shall take appropriate action normally within thirty days of receipt of the report. Such action shall include:
(i) a statement concerning the facts of the matter; and
(ii) recommendations to one or more Parties or any other ruling which it deems appropriate.

8. If a Party to which recommendations are addressed considers itself unable to implement them, it should promptly furnish reasons in writing to the Committee. In that event, the Committee shall consider what further action may be appropriate.

9. If the Committee considers that the circumstances are serious enough to justify such action, it may authorize one or more Parties to suspend the application to any other Party or Parties of such obligations under this Agreement as it determines to be appropriate in the circumstances.

10. The Committee shall keep under surveillance any matter on which it has made recommendations or given rulings.

11. If a dispute arises between Parties relating to rights and obligations under this Agreement, Parties should complete the dispute settlement procedures under this Agreement before availing themselves of any rights which they have under the GATT, including invoking Article XXIII thereof.

PART III

SPECIAL AND DIFFERENTIAL TREATMENT

Article 21

1. Developing country Parties may delay application of its provisions for a period not exceeding five years from the date of entry into force of this Agreement for such countries. Developing country Parties who choose to delay application of this Agreement shall notify the Director-General to the CONTRACTING PARTIES to the GATT accordingly.

2. In addition to paragraph 1 above, developing country Parties may delay application of Article 1.2. *(b)* (iii) and Article 6 for a period not exceeding three years following their application of all other provisions of this Agreement. Developing country Parties that choose to delay application of the provisions specified in this paragraph shall notify the Director-General to the CONTRACTING PARTIES to the GATT accordingly.

3. Developed country Parties shall furnish, on mutually agreed terms, technical assistance to developing country Parties that so request. On this basis developed country Parties shall draw up programmes of technical assistance which may include, *inter alia*, training of personnel, assistance in preparing implementation measures, access to sources of information regarding customs valuation methodology, and advice on the application of the provisions of this Agreement.

PART IV

FINAL PROVISIONS

Acceptance and accession

Article 22

1. This Agreement shall be open for acceptance by signature or otherwise by governments contracting parties to the GATT and by the European Economic Community.

2. This Agreement shall be open for acceptance by signature or otherwise by governments having provisionally acceded to the GATT, on terms related to the effective application of rights and obligations under this Agreement, which take into account rights and obligations in the instruments providing for their provisional accession.

3. This Agreement shall be open to accession by any other government on terms, related to the effective application of rights and obligations under this Agreement, to be agreed between that government and the Parties, by the deposit with the Director-General to the CONTRACTING PARTIES to the GATT of an instrument of accession which states the terms so agreed.

4. In regard to acceptance, the provisions of Article XXVI: 5.*a* and *b* of the General Agreement would be applicable.

Reservations

Article 23

Reservations may not be entered in respect of any of the provisions of this Agreement without the consent of the other Parties.

Entry into force

Article 24

This Agreement shall enter into force on 1 January 1981 for the governments[1] which have accepted or acceded to it by that date. For each other government it shall enter into force on the thirtieth day following the date of its acceptance or accession to this Agreement.

National legislation

Article 25

1. Each government accepting or acceding to this Agreement shall ensure, not later than the date of entry into force of this Agreement for it, the conformity of its laws, regulations and administrative procedures with the provisions of this Agreement.

2. Each Party shall inform the Committee of any changes in its laws and regulations relevant to this Agreement and in the administration of such laws and regulations.

Review

Article 26

The Committee shall review annually the implementation and operation of this Agreement taking into account the objectives thereof. The Committee shall annually inform the CONTRACTING PARTIES to the GATT of developments during the period covered by such reviews.

1. The term 'governments' is deemed to include the competent authorities of the European Economic Community.

Amendments

Article 27

The Parties may amend this Agreement, having regard, *inter alia,* to the experience gained in its implementation. Such an amendment, once the Parties have concurred in accordance with procedures established by the Committee, shall not come into force for any Party until it has been accepted by such Party.

Withdrawal

Article 28

Any Party may withdraw from this Agreement. The withdrawal shall take effect upon the expiration of sixty days from the date on which written notice of withdrawal is received by the Director-General to the CONTRACTING PARTIES to the GATT. Any Party may, upon the receipt of such notice, request an immediate meeting of the Committee.

Secretariat

Article 29

This Agreement shall be serviced by the GATT secretariat except in regard to those responsibilities specifically assigned to the Technical Committee, which will be serviced by the secretariat of the Customs Co-operation Council.

Deposit

Article 30

This Agreement shall be deposited with the Director-General to the CONTRACTING PARTIES to the GATT, who shall promptly furnish to each Party and each contracting party to the GATT a certified copy thereof and of each amendment thereto pursuant to Article 27, and a notification of each acceptance thereof or accession thereto pursuant to Article 22 and of each withdrawal therefrom pursuant to Article 28.

FINAL PROVISIONS

Registration

Article 31

This Agreement shall be registered in accordance with the provisions of Article 102 of the Charter of the United Nations.

Done at Geneva this twelfth day of April nineteen hundred and seventy-nine in a single copy, in the English, French and Spanish languages, each text being authentic.

Annex 4. The Protocol

(PROTOCOL TO THE AGREEMENT ON IMPLEMENTATION OF ARTICLE VII OF THE GENERAL AGREEMENT ON TARIFFS AND TRADE)

The Parties to the Agreement on Implementation of Article VII of the General Agreement on Tariffs and Trade (hereinafter referred to as 'the Agreement').

Having regard to the Multilateral Trade Negotiations and to the desire expressed by the Trade Negotiations Committee at its meeting of 11 and 12 April 1979 to arrive at a single text of an Agreement on Implementation of Article VII of the General Agreement on Tariffs and Trade;

Recognizing that developing countries may have particular problems in applying the Agreement;

Considering that the provisions of Article 27 of the Agreement relating to amendments have not yet entered into force;

Hereby:

I

1. *Agree* to the deletion of the provision of Article 1.2.(*b*)(iv) of the Agreement;

2. *Recognize* that the five-year delay in the application of the provisions of the Agreement by developing countries provided for in Article 21.1 may, in practice, be insufficient for certain developing countries. In such cases a developing country Party to the Agreement may request before the end of the period referred to in Article 21.1 an extension of such period, it being understood that the Parties to the Agreement will give sympathetic consideration to such a request in cases where the developing country in question can show good cause;

3. *Recognize* that developing countries which currently value goods on the

basis of officially established minimum values may wish to make a reservation to enable them to retain such values on a limited and transitional basis under such terms and conditions as may be agreed to by the Parties to the Agreement;

4. *Recognize* that developing countries which consider that the reversal of the sequential order at the request of the importer provided for in Article 4 of the Agreement may give rise to real difficulties for them may wish to make a reservation to Article 4 in the following terms:

> 'The Government of .... reserves the right to provide that the relevant provision of Article 4 of the Agreement shall apply only when the customs authorities agree to the request to reverse the order of Articles 5 and 6.'

If developing countries make such a reservation, the Parties to the Agreement shall consent to it under Article 23 or the Agreement;

5. *Recognize* that developing countries may wish to make a reservation with respect to Article 5.2 of the Agreement in the following terms:

> 'The Government of .... reserves the right to provide that Article 5.2 of the Agreement shall be applied in accordance with the provisions of the relevant note thereto whether or not the importer so requests.'

If developing countries make such a reservation, the Parties to the Agreement shall consent to it under Article 23 of the Agreement;

6. *Recognize* that certain developing countries have expressed concern that there may be problems in the implementation of Article 1 of the Agreement insofar as it relates to importations into their countries by sole agents, sole distributors and sole concessionaires. The Parties to the Agreement agree that, if such problems arise in practice in developing countries applying the Agreement, a study of this question shall be made, at the request of such countries, with a view to finding appropriate solutions;

7. *Agree* that Article 17 recognizes that in applying the Agreement, customs administrations may need to make enquiries concerning the truth or accuracy of any statement, document or declaration presented to them for customs valuation purposes. They further agree that the Article thus acknowledges that enquiries may be made which are, for example, aimed at verifying that the elements of value declared or presented to customs in connection with a determination of customs value are complete and correct. They recognize that Par-

ties to the Agreement, subject to their national laws and procedures, have the right to expect the full co-operation of importers in these enquiries;

8. *Agree* that the price actually paid or payable includes all payments actually made or to be made as a condition of sale of the imported goods, by the buyer to the seller, or by the buyer to a third party to satisfy an obligation of the seller.

II

1. Upon the entry into force of the Agreement the provisions of this Protocol shall be deemed to be part of the Agreement.

2. This Protocol shall be deposited with the Director-General to the CONTRACTING PARTIES to the GATT. It is open for acceptance, by signature or otherwise, by signatories of the Agreement on Implementation of Article VII of the General Agreement on Tariffs and Trade and by other governments accepting or acceding to the Agreement pursuant to the provisions of Article 22 thereof.

Done at Geneva this first day of November 1979 in a single copy in the English, French and Spanish languages, each text being authentic.

fenedex

Fenedex, Federation for the Netherlands export, set up in 1954, is a non-profit, private organization, independent and unsubsidized with the aim to promote Dutch export in general and its members' export in particular.

Fenedex has about 800 members, therefore the secretariat is able to gather and exchange a lot of practical export know-how which can be used to the advantage of the individual member.

Fenedex' primary task is supporting members in their activities on foreign markets.

Next to the individual support, Fenedex organizes a number of courses, seminars and discussion meetings in order to accomplish a collective transference of practical information to industrial circles, members and non-members and to exchange experience and know-how gained in the course of export transactions.

The progressing internationalization-process demands a more specialized know-how, particularly of non-specific commercial subjects like fiscal and legal affairs and staff problems. This development requires that Fenedex can give rapid, efficient support and assistance on many export matters.

Fenedex is a member of the International Association of Institutes of Export (I.A.I.E.), which aims to develop ideas and to exchange know-how and experience in the field of export training.

Address:
Fenedex,
Bezuidenhoutseweg 76a,
2594 AW THE HAGUE.
tel.: 070 - 83 81 08.
telex: 33040.

GPSR Compliance

The European Union's (EU) General Product Safety Regulation (GPSR) is a set of rules that requires consumer products to be safe and our obligations to ensure this.

If you have any concerns about our products, you can contact us on ProductSafety@springernature.com

In case Publisher is established outside the EU, the EU authorized representative is:

Springer Nature Customer Service Center GmbH
Europaplatz 3
69115 Heidelberg, Germany

Batch number: 10824476

Printed by Printforce, the Netherlands